The Wandering Sage

The Wandering Sage

Spiritual stories from
around the world

Retold by
Robert Van de Weyer

BOOKS

Winchester, UK
New York, USA

Copyright © 2004 O Books
46A West Street, Alresford, Hants SO24 9AU, U.K.
Tel: +44 (0) 1962 736880 Fax: +44 (0) 1962 736881
E-mail: office@johnhunt-publishing.com
www.0-books.net

U.S. office:
240 West 35th Street, Suite 500
New York, NY 10001
E-mail: obooks@aol.com

Text: © Robert Van de Weyer 2004

Design: Nautilus Design, Basingstoke, UK

ISBN 1 903816 65 3

A CIP catalogue record for this book is available from the British
Library.

Printed in Singapore by Tien Wah Press (Pte) Ltd

◆

CONTENTS

Preface 8

Introduction 13

Measuring intelligence *Sufi* 22

Apples and strawberries *Hasidic* 23

The sound of money *Celtic* 24

A dream about a butterfly *Taoist* 25

A knotted tree *Taoist* 27

A dustpan and broom *Sufi* 29

Stolen goods *Hasidic* 31

Fish in the river *Taoist* 33

A scholar in a storm *Sufi* 34

A home for the elderly *Taoist* 35

A stolen ornament *Hasidic* 37

The triumph of light *Celtic* 38

Violent entertainment *Taoist* 40

A melon in winter *Sufi* 42

A dispute over meat *Taoist* 44

Welcome for a singer *Sufi* 46

A beautiful scratch *Hasidic* 47

Honey from the pot *Celtic* 48

Home town *Taoist* 49

Earthen pitchers *Hasidic* 51

Thoughts of wrestling *Taoist* 52

A nobleman's gold *Sufi* 54

Chasing the sun *Taoist* 55

◆

Race for land *Celtic* *57*

Catching a fish *Taoist* *59*

Unwelcome visitors *Sufi* *61*

Preparations for archery *Taoist* *62*

Old twins *Taoist* *63*

Natural treasure *Sufi* *64*

The death of a son *Taoist* *66*

Passage of life *Hasidic* *67*

Children in a burning house *Taoist* *68*

A perfect reflection *Sufi* *70*

Green salve *Taoist* *72*

A king's dignity *Sufi* *74*

Adulterated honey *Hasidic* *75*

The grieving widow *Celtic* *77*

A merchant's dilemma *Hasidic* *78*

Trees for the future *Celtic* *80*

A blow on the cheek *Hasidic* *81*

Powerful words *Sufi* *82*

The window and the mirror *Hasidic* *83*

Dreams of change *Taoist* *84*

A generous inheritance *Celtic* *86*

Clever tricks *Taoist* *88*

A beautiful estate *Taoist* *89*

A carpenter's dream *Sufi* *90*

A lazy shadow *Taoist* *91*

Food for clothes *Sufi* *92*

◆

A young man's aims *Taoist* *93*

Tranquility amid noise *Hasidic* *94*

Three desires *Sufi* *95*

Constant vigilance *Sufi* *96*

The beggar and the merchant *Taoist* *97*

A chest of suspicion *Sufi* *98*

Valuable merchandise *Hasidic* *100*

A call to war *Taoist* *101*

The truth of ignorance *Sufi* *102*

The sweetest sound *Hasidic* *103*

A robber as king *Sufi* *105*

Passing on a secret *Sufi* *107*

Palmistry and magic *Sufi* *108*

The rich man and the poor man *Hasidic* . . . *110*

Wisdom from cleaning *Sufi* *111*

A jeweled cap *Sufi* *112*

An unhappy town *Taoist* *113*

Cat and mouse *Celtic* *114*

Blindness to truth *Sufi* *115*

Two chief ministers *Taoist* *117*

True ownership *Celtic* *119*

The mountain path *Sufi* *121*

Money for flattery *Hasidic* *123*

Medical advice *Taoist* *124*

Wisdom for a fool *Celtic* *125*

Sources *127*

◆

Preface

In the footsteps of the Wandering Sage

When I think of the Wandering Sage, I sometimes imagine him in the Sufi heartlands of the Middle East. I first encountered Sufism during a long visit to Afghanistan in the spring of 1969. Owing to the final disintegration of the ancient vehicle in which I was travelling, I was stranded for a week in the desert between Herat and Kandahar. Happily the vehicle was able to freewheel down a mountain road to a group of mud huts in a valley that functioned as a primitive motel. One evening a wandering Sufi arrived at the motel's dining-area – a large room with rugs on the floor and an open fire in the middle – and entertained the guests with stories and aphorisms. I can still visualise this man's leathery face, dried and wrinkled by the summer sun and the winter gales, and his darting eyes that had turned red with the sand constantly blowing into them.

However in the intervening years the Middle East has suffered a succession of political whirlwinds. I like to think that Sufis continue to walk from one town and village to another, ignoring the military encampments and the terrorist gangs. If they do there is little prospect of innocent travellers from the West hearing their words. So, for the time being at least, we cannot follow the wandering sage in that part of the world.

In the late 1960s China was caught up in the whirlwind of the Cultural Revolution, unleashed by Chairman Mao. Later in 1969 I took a course in Chinese philosophy, and first encountered the great Taoist thinkers. I yearned to travel to China, and see for myself the land on which they trod. But, even though in my foolhardy youth I should happily have risked my life, visas were impossible to obtain. Now the Chinese

◆

government is eager to attract tourists and many of the sights associated with Taoism are easy to visit. As a visitor, I would try to imagine Lao Tzu and Chuang Tzu making paradoxical remarks to the local population, and doing peculiar and unexpected things in order to illustrate their teaching. Unfortunately, however, I sense that arriving in the Taoist heartlands by long haul flight would rob the visit of its spiritual power. Or perhaps I just want to keep my imagination unsullied by experience.

In any event, the place where the western traveller can most conveniently tread in the Wandering Sage's footsteps, and can most readily conjure up images of him, is Ireland. My first Irish sage was neither a wanderer nor a man. She was Gertrude, the hugely fat elderly woman who cooked for my bachelor uncle near Dublin. When in the 1950s my parents took me to stay with Uncle Charlie, I used to find my way to the kitchen, where Gertrude fed me with fruitcake and told me stories. I later discovered many of these stories in collections made by scholars who visited remote Irish communities in the nineteenth century. I doubt if Gertrude ever read these collections, so I assume she heard the stories in the manner that they had been handed down for century upon century – in front of a smouldering peat fire on dark winter evenings. And, of course, many of the stories centred on a Wandering Sage.

After a week or so with Uncle Charlie, these family holidays usually involved a tour of various relatives and friends. These were mainly decaying members of the Anglo-Irish aristocracy, and they lived in vast, cold and decaying houses. In many cases they had retreated to one wing of the house, leaving the rest to mice and spiders; and they were served by ancient and loyal butlers and footmen, housekeepers and chambermaids. After breakfast each day we set out with a

◆

packed lunch and a flask of tea in our Morris Traveller, a car built like a Tudor house with wooden beams, and we visited many of the sites associated with those sages whose names are remembered. So these places and Gertrude's stories coalesced in my mind to form a composite picture of the life of the Wandering Sage.

If you are an adult, I cannot promise you the same imaginative experiences that I enjoyed as a child. Nor can I promise you that the places I visited as a child, most of which were remote and overgrown, will be the same. On the contrary, many of them have been adapted for the tourists that now come to Ireland in large numbers; and the countryside around them has in some cases been punctuated by the Mediterranean-style villas that prosperous Irish families currently favour. Nonetheless, they mostly retain their capacity to stir the soul, bringing peace or disturbance depending on what you need at the time. So let me recommend a few to you.

South of Dublin is Glendalough, where a sage called Kevin lived. It is a wooded valley with two deep lakes, ringed by mountains. It seem that Kevin settled here when his bones and muscles grew too old for the wandering life, and initially made his home on the banks of the lower lake. But once his presence there became widely known, a steady stream of people arrived to listen to his wisdom. While he was usually happy to oblige, he also needed a place of quiet retreat, so he disappeared from time to time to the upper lake. The somewhat dubious remains of his second cell can be seen near the bridge. There has long been a cathedral at Glendalough, which boasts a fine round tower characteristic of ancient Irish churches – an architectural style that the Christians may have adopted from their pagan forbears. Incidentally, on the way to Glandalough you can pop in to see Powerscourt, the

◆

finest Georgian house in Ireland that is also one of my ancestral homes.

Another outing from Dublin is to Kildare. It is associated with Brigid, a semi πmythical figure whom the Christians regard as a saint, but who may have lived in pre-Christian times – if she lived at all. She is famous for her intelligence and ready wit in conversation. She lived in the Curragh, a large area of unfenced common land to the east of the town. At one stage she may have had some kind of community there, and each evening she is said to have wandered round the muddy lanes nearby, inviting travellers to come and stay with her. Kildare literally means 'place of the oak', and is named after the oak tree under whose boughs she built a hut for herself.

A third outing from Dublin is to Tara and Kells. Tara is the ancient capital of Ireland, and the kings of Ireland welcomed Wandering Sages to their court to hear what they had to say. Patrick, Ireland's patron saint, began his work of converting the Irish to Christianity by coming to Tara and preaching to the King; he also performed a number of miracles to demonstrate the power of his faith. There are no buildings at Tara, but the extensive earthworks mark the site of the capital. Kells is associated with the greatest of Ireland's Christian Wandering Sages, Columba. He composed songs and told parables in order to convey his message, and he formed an order of travelling bards that was based here. Kells cathedral has a round tower, and the churchyard contains two Celtic crosses.

In addition to the hinterland of Dublin, the other main area for this kind of site is the Dingle peninsula. On the north coast of the peninsula is Mount Brandon. This is especially associated with the Christian wanderer, Brendan, who journeyed by open boat with twelve companions to Iceland and Newfoundland, returning via the Azores. His astonishing

◆

trip was recounted in a book that became an early medieval bestseller across Europe. Brendan went up this mountain for the forty days and nights of Lent in order to prepare himself spiritually. One can readily imagine that the mountain, which rises spectacularly from the sea, provided a place of retreat for numerous sages both before and since.

Dingle also contains the Gallarus Oratory, the best-preserved ancient Celtic building in the whole of Britain. It is rectangular, about four metres by six, and built by corbelling, in which each stone course is smaller than the one beneath, so the courses eventually meet at the top to form a roof. It is normally assumed that this was a place of prayer and religious ceremony. If so, it was surely also a place where people met to listen to the sages that wandered around Ireland in both pre-Christian and Christian times.

On the road from Dublin to Dingle, just before reaching Athlone, there is Clonmacnois. It stands on the banks of the River Shannon, and in medieval times became one of Ireland's largest monasteries; there are some fine ruins. In an earlier period it is said that a wanderer called Piran lived here, gathering around him a community of wild animals. Piran then set off to the south-east coast, built himself a coracle, and launched out into the sea. The winds and currents took him to the north coast of Cornwall, where he established another animal community.

◆

INTRODUCTION

Stories and characters

In every society known to historians, and in every culture studied by anthropologists, there is a fund of stories – parables, fables, legends – which encapsulate moral and spiritual values, and pass those values from one generation to the next. These stories are meant both to capture the listener's attention as amusing or exciting, and also to convey a profound inner meaning. Characters, objects, or situations from them are used as easy and precise metaphors. So, in countries with a Christian tradition people frequently refer to "the good Samaritan," "the prodigal son," "the lost sheep," and "the wise virgins," expecting their listeners to know exactly what they mean. Sometimes these references become so familiar that metaphor and meaning conflate; "talents," for example, does not now primarily refer to coins, but means "abilities," for which in Christ's parable it was an image.

Whereas in novels and plays the characters are usually quite complex with several facets, the characters in these moral and spiritual stories are usually simple, representing some particular quality. This is most manifest in stories where the characters are animals: a fox may represent cunning, a hen guileless simplicity, and an owl wisdom. Where the characters are human, a person's profession or station is often the key: a knight is typically bold, a merchant greedy, a priest hypocritical, and a peasant honest. Occasionally an animal or human acts contrary to expectations, thereby achieving dramatic effect, but these exceptions serve only to prove the rule.

◆

◆

The character of the wandering sage

One of the characters who makes a frequent appearance in moral and spiritual stories across the world, and who is undoubtedly the most intelligent, is the wandering sage. Sometimes he has a name: he is Mulla Nasrudin, for example, in some Sufi tales from the Middle East and a name given to him in south India is Guru Nudel. More often he is nameless. He appears to have no past and no relatives. He is simultaneously young and old: he is young enough to walk great distances, and to be quite agile at times, but he is old enough to possess great wisdom, and to command immediate respect. He has no home and no money, and carries no possessions. He is often given accommodation and food but, when he sets out on a journey, he is unconcerned about what he might eat and where he might sleep. Although people may give him some honorific title, such as mulla or guru, he belongs to no religious hierarchy, and has no religious affiliation.

In relation to the stories in which he appears, he has four crucial abilities. First, he has an uncanny knack of appearing on a scene just when he is needed. This may be when people have tried hard to solve a problem, but have failed, or when someone is about to do something exceedingly foolish, or when someone's behavior has become utterly intolerable. He also knows precisely when to leave. Far from wanting to dominate people, he wants people to take control of their own lives and when he has done just enough to enable them to do this, he departs.

Second, he has an extremely quick wit. When people are anxious or confused, his words are gentle and patient. But when people are puffed up with pride, treating others with contempt, he knows how to puncture them with a single

◆

phrase. And when they are angry, he knows how to deflect their rage. Sometimes he uses verbal jokes to convey a message. These are not jokes that generate laughter, but they are flashes of humor that cause jaws to drop and minds to stop.

Third, he often teaches people by asking them questions. He often leads people through a series of questions until they reach the right answer for themselves. He uses this technique to help people untangle moral and emotional muddles; and he also uses it as a means of reconciling enemies.

Fourth, he likes, wherever possible, to make his points by creating situations. He is adept at manipulating people into circumstances where their habitual behavior is shown to be absurd or plain wrong. He also likes to turn people's greed, callousness, or other vices against them, so they learn the consequences of their own evil. And he sometimes takes advantage of people's folly, not for his own advantage, but to show them how to be wise. He calculates that salutary experiences are far more memorable than fine words.

Spiritual traditions

Although he can be found in many cultures, there are four spiritual traditions where the wandering sage is especially prominent. One is Taoism in China. Two of the three great Taoist philosophers, Chuang Tzu and Lieh Tzu, traveled from place to place. The books carrying their names are collections of conversations, discourses, and incidents associated with them. In some of the incidents they themselves appear as wandering sages, setting up situations in order to make a point; and in some of their discourses they tell stories about other wandering sages. Indeed, those incidents and stories are interchangeable, leading some scholars to conclude that

◆

Chuang Tzu and Lieh Tzu are mythical figures: they are simply archetypal wandering sages who have been given names.

Another tradition is Sufism. The Sufi movement began late in the eighth century in reaction to the growing religious power of the Muslim clergy and lawyers. Men and women dressed in rough woolen clothes – the word suf probably means wool – went to live in remote caves and huts, or walked from place to place, in the hope of attaining inner serenity. Some of them became hugely popular, and their advice was eagerly sought. They told stories as a means of teaching spiritual truth and some of these stories concerned the sages like themselves. Stories were often told about them. Again, the two types of stories were virtually interchangeable. Among the greatest of the Sufi storytellers was Rumi, who was born in Afghanistan early in the fourth century, and traveled throughout the Middle East and his contemporary Sadi, who came from Iran and wandered through India, central Asia and even Africa.

The Celtic tradition of Ireland is another source of wandering sage tales. It used to be assumed that Celts came over from continental Europe to populate Britain and Ireland; modern scholars are more inclined to think that the indigenous population was merely influenced by Celtic ideas and art. In any event, Ireland's relative isolation enabled its ancient culture to survive; and when scholars in the nineteenth century, mainly from England, learnt the Irish language and visited rural areas, they discovered that the peasants had a rich fund of stories, handed down orally from one generation to the next. Many of these stories concern wandering sages.

Modern Jews, especially in America, are famous for their sharp wit that derives directly from the Hasidic tradition of

◆

eastern Europe. Hasidism arose in the Jewish communities of Poland and Lithuania in the late eighteenth century and, like Sufism, it was in part a reaction to the legalism of the established religious leadership. It encouraged joy and humor and it revolved around zaddikim, who were charismatic spiritual leaders, often possessing a strong sense of irony. The zaddikim themselves told stories about past sages, and their own behavior generated new stories. Most Hasidic centers in Europe were destroyed by the Nazi holocaust but fortunately many followers of Hasidism had already migrated to America, where the tradition survives and flourishes.

The style of the stories

Spiritual stories are usually related very simply and starkly, containing only such information as is necessary to the plot. The parables of Jesus are models of this minimalist style. No doubt when grandparents told these stories sitting by the open fire on dark evenings, they embroidered them with details that connected them more closely to their grandchildren's experiences. Sometimes when they are retold in modern books, they are greatly lengthened. But brevity heightens their power, as Jesus well understood: by focusing only on the salient events, the message is made clear.

Brevity is a particular virtue when the central character is the wandering sage. We all know from experience that when someone pads out a joke with unnecessary asides, the joke loses its impact. Since many of the wandering sage stories are, in reality, sophisticated jokes, the same applies.

One happy consequence of their brevity is that wandering sage stories travel well. It requires no knowledge whatever of Chinese culture to appreciate stories from Chuang Tzu.

◆

You may be ignorant of Islam yet still enjoy any of Rumi's tales. Indeed, it is impossible from the stories themselves to distinguish their origin and some very similar stories crop up in two or more traditions.

Identity

The wandering sage is invariably referred to as "he" but he is really sexless. He has no attitudes that mark him out as male or female, and he never relates to people in terms of their sex. The fact of his wandering freely suggests maleness, simply because female mendicants are virtually unknown, whereas male mendicants in many parts of the world have been quite common. But if there were in English a personal pronoun that had no gender, this would be more appropriate.

More often than not the wandering sage is nameless, and is referred to simply as the sage. I follow this custom.

Sources

When people re-tell stories, even if they wish to be entirely faithful to their source, they may feel impelled to make minor alterations to make them more comprehensible to their particular listeners or readers. In the following collection I have followed this time-honored practice and I make no apology. The sources from which I have derived these stories are ancient enough yet the original source for each story is, I am sure, far more ancient still, and can never be known. A good spiritual story is like a species of plant or animal in that it has evolved slowly over a very long time.

These are my sources. The Taoist stories are mostly taken from the books of Chuang Tzu and Lieh Tzu; one is taken from the Lotus Sutra, which is revered by both Buddhists and Taoists. The Sufi stories mainly come from the writings of Rumi and Sadi. The Hasidic stories come from anthologies

◆

by Louis Newman, Lewis Browne, and Nathan Ausubel, each of which draws on several sources. The Celtic stories come partly from the collections of Douglas Hyde, and partly from my own memory. As a child half a century ago I spent many of my vacations staying in large decaying mansions in Ireland, where I listened eagerly to the stories told by old estate workers and house servants. It is to them and their kind – the human storehouses of spiritual stories – that this book is dedicated.

Religious unity

In their doctrines and creeds the religions of the world differ and disagree and these disagreements often provoke mutual hostility, which sometimes leads to violence and bloodshed. Since these doctrines and creeds purport to express some ultimate truth, and since ultimate truth – if it exists – must be beyond human understanding and definition, these differences and disagreements are manifestly absurd.

The rituals and symbols of the religions of the world also differ: the adherents of one religion, or sect within a religion, often look with bemused contempt at the symbols and rituals of other religions and sects. Since rituals and symbols are largely a matter of taste, and since taste is to a great extent formed by culture, this contempt is no less than bigotry.

The wandering sage rarely mentions doctrines and creeds and, when he does, it is only to ridicule them. He treats all rituals and symbols with respect, thus he is a figure of global religious unity.

Robert Van de Weyer

◆

The Wandering Sage

◆

Measuring intelligence

A man was acknowledged as having the most intelligent brain in his town. Unfortunately he had become proud and arrogant, and treated other people in the town with contempt.

The sage arrived in the town, and sat down in the town square. Seeing a newcomer, the intelligent man walked over to him and engaged him in conversation, in order to assert his superiority. The sage quickly recognized what the intelligent man was trying to do, and allowed him to show off his mental powers.

Then the sage rose to his feet, picked up a stick that was lying on the ground, and hit the intelligent man gently on the head. The intelligent man flushed with anger, and picked up another stick.

"You can hit me as hard as you wish," the sage said, "if you first answer a simple question." "Very well," the intelligent man replied, confident that he could easily answer any question the sage might devise.

"When I hit you," the sage asked, "did the sound come from the stick that I used, or from your skull?" The intelligent man had no answer.

"Let me ask you another question," the sage said, "and if you can answer this correctly, I shall bow down at your feet in homage." "Very well," the intelligent man replied, excited at the prospect of the sage bowing down before him.

"Is your superior mind revealed by the intelligent remarks that you make," the sage asked, "or by the unintelligent remarks that others make?" The intelligent man had no answer; but he understood the question sufficiently to know that he should treat other people with respect.

Sufi

◆

◆

Apples and strawberries

The sage was walking through the countryside when a young man caught him up. "May I walk with you?" the young man asked. "By all means," the sage replied.

They walked in silence together for a few minutes. Then the young man said, "If you are as wise as people say that you are, then you can summarize morality in a single sentence." "Morality is easy to understand," the sage replied, "but hard to practice." "If I am to practice it," the young man said, "then I must begin by understanding it." "Very well," the sage said. "Morality consists in not doing to others what you would not want others to do to you."

Later that day the sage and the young man passed an orchard. The young man picked several apples and satisfied his hunger, but the sage took none. Some hours later they passed a field where strawberries were growing. The young man picked enough to satisfy his hunger, but the sage took none. The young man asked the sage why he was taking nothing but the sage remained silent.

On the following day they passed another orchard, and the young man picked some apples. But this time the sage seized the apples, and started to eat them himself. The young man was taken aback, but said nothing. Later they passed another strawberry field, and the young man helped himself. The sage seized the strawberries. The young man now reacted with anger, and tried to seize them back.

The sage smiled, and said: "You think nothing of taking apples and strawberries belonging to a farmer, but are angry when someone takes apples and strawberries that you regard as your own." The young man hung his head in shame. The sage put his arm on his shoulder, and repeated his words from the previous day: "Morality is easy to understand, but hard to practice."

Hasidic

◆

◆

The sound of money

The sage arrived in a town on the busiest day of the month, when families from all over the region came to sell their wares and buy what they needed. The public square was packed with men, women, and children, and the sound of their voices was deafening.

A wealthy merchant asked the sage what he was selling. "I have nothing to offer except my words," the sage replied. "Words are worthless," the merchant said. "Words of love are worth more than all the gold in the world," the sage replied. "To prove your point," the merchant said, "show me that people are willing to pay for your wise words." "Very well," the sage said. "Lend me a large coin." The merchant handed the sage his largest silver coin.

The sage climbed onto the merchant's stall, lifted the coin high above his head, and dropped it onto the cobbles below. It landed with a loud clink. At the sound of the coin the crowd fell silent, and turned toward the sage.

"You have ears to hear the sound of money," the sage said. "Let me tell you about something worth much more than money." The sage then spoke with great eloquence about love. People were so moved by his words that, when he had finished, they begged him to tell them how they could show love. "Be generous to the poor," he replied. So they put coins on the stall where he was standing, and asked him to use the coins for the benefit of the poor.

The merchant was now ashamed of himself, and from his own wealth he doubled the amount that the people had given. The sage used the money to build a large house where the poor could come for food and shelter. And the people continued to give money to maintain the house.

Celtic

◆

◆

A dream about a butterfly

There was a self-important man who sat in the tavern every evening, and offered his opinions on any and every subject that came into his head. He also enjoyed talking about himself and his experiences. He spoke in such a loud voice that people couldn't help hearing him and he never doubted that people were interested in what he had to say. If people disagreed with him, he dismissed their opinions with contempt.

The sage came into the tavern, ordered a mug of beer, and sat down in a corner drinking it. The self-important man was giving his views on some topical matters. Then, as usual, he started talking about himself: "Last night I had a most interesting dream. I dreamt I was a butterfly, flapping my wings and flying from flower to flower. I thought like a butterfly, and I felt like a butterfly. It seemed utterly real. Then I woke up, and realized that it was only a dream – and that I'm really me!"

A voice came from the corner of the tavern: "How do you know that you're you? You could really be a butterfly, and being a man might only be a dream." The self-important man turned round and stared at the sage. As he tried to give an answer, he started to splutter; he couldn't think of what to say. His face went bright red, and he marched out of the tavern.

For several days the self-important man stayed away from the tavern. He wandered round the town, muttering to himself: "Am I a butterfly, or am I me?" Meanwhile the other people in the tavern were able to talk happily among themselves, sharing their opinions freely.

Finally the sage went up to the man, and said: "Everything is a matter of personal opinion, even your own existence.

◆

◆

Come back to the tavern." The man came back. And from that day onward he was as happy to listen to other people's opinions as he was to give his own.

Taoist

◆

◆

A knotted tree

There was a town where everyone was constantly busy. The people worked hard every day, and often continued working in the evening. There were no days of rest or festivals. No one ever visited another person's home for a meal and a drink, nor did they meet at taverns – so there was not a single tavern in the entire place. And they never stopped one another in the street for a chat; people merely rushed from one place to another as their business required. As a result of all this effort the town was very rich. But no one took time to enjoy this wealth; everyone looked gaunt, gray, and weary – and no one ever smiled.

The sage arrived in the town, and observed its frantic activity. In the middle of the town there was a small park where he noticed several tree stumps, but only one tree still standing. He walked beside a young man who was rushing by, and asked about the tree stumps and the tree. "Most of the trees were cut down to make tools and carts and other useful things," the young man said, "but the remaining tree is so knotted that no carpenter can saw it, and its branches are so twisted that they can't even be turned into handles."

The sage went into the park, and sat under the tree. He remained there for three months. At first people were so absorbed in their own affairs that they ignored him. But they couldn't help noticing this strange figure out of the corner of their eyes and soon his laziness started to irritate them. Eventually his presence was mentioned at the monthly meeting of the town council and it was decided that the mayor and councilors should go and speak to him.

So the following day the mayor put on his chain and robes of office, and, followed by his councilors, marched to the

◆

park. "Why are you sitting under the tree?" the mayor asked the sage. "In order to enjoy its shade," the sage replied. "Why do you not take a job and make yourself useful?" the mayor asked. "Because I wish to live a long time," the sage replied. "I don't understand," the major retorted.

"Look at this tree," the sage said with a smile. "It's so knotted and twisted that it's useless. Yet, while the useful trees have all been cut down, this useless tree survives."

The mayor and the councilors were astonished and soon the sage's words were being repeated throughout the town. People stopped working so hard. They visited each other's homes and chatted in the street, and taverns opened where they met in the evenings. The mayor declared that certain days were days of rest, when people should relax completely and on some of these days they had festivals. The town became somewhat poorer but, to their own surprise, the people started smiling.

Taoist

◆

◆

A dustpan and broom

The sage saw an old man tottering down a street. The old man was so unsteady on his feet, and his hand trembled so violently on his stick, that he was in danger of falling over with every step. The sage went up to him, and offered to hold him by the arm as he walked. But the old man's face flushed with anger, and he pushed the sage aside. "I can look after myself," he declared. "I don't need any help. Mind your own business!"

"If you talk like that to everyone," the sage said, "you must be very lonely." The old man grunted loudly, and continued on his way; the sage followed a few paces behind.

The old man went into the goldsmith's shop, and took out a large bag of gold filings. The sage also went into the goldsmith's shop, and stood beside the old man. "If you're determined to be useful," the old man said grumpily, "fetch me some scales so I can weigh my gold." "I'll fetch a broom," the sage replied.

"Don't talk nonsense," the old man said; "do as I say, and fetch some scales." "I'll fetch a dustpan as well," the sage replied. The old man was now so annoyed that he lifted up his stick in order to hit the sage. But as he did so, he fell backward onto the ground.

The sage knelt beside him, and offered to lift him to his feet. "Since it's your fault that I fell," the old man said, "it's your duty to pick me up." As soon as the old man was standing again, he said to the sage: "Why do you talk of a broom and a dustpan when I ask for scales?"

The sage smiled and said: "Your hands tremble so much that you will spill the gold filings as you pour them onto the scales. So you will undoubtedly need a broom and a dustpan to collect the filings from the floor."

◆

◆

The old man's anger turned to tears. "Come to my house and be my servant," the old man cried. "I need someone who knows what I need before I have to ask for it." "As soon you can accept help with grace," the sage replied, "then all your neighbors will be your servants. Everyone can see what you need and everyone loves to be needed." The sage then helped the old man to walk back to his house.

The old man now began to smile and talk pleasantly to his neighbors and they took pleasure in doing whatever he needed. Whenever he observed that one of his neighbors lacked something, he used some of his gold to buy it for them. So as death grew closer, he became steadily poorer and happier.

Sufi

◆

Stolen goods

A certain town had numerous thieves, and they were causing great distress. The town judge gave harsh sentences to every thief that was brought before him. But, since thieves are very skilled at avoiding detection, the local constables only captured very few.

The sage visited the town. The judge and the constables came to him, and asked his advice on how they could stop the robberies. "There is nothing you can do to stop them," the sage replied. The judge and the constables hung their heads in despair. "The only people who can stop the robberies," the sage continued, "are the people themselves." The judge and the constables were baffled.

The sage told them to convene a meeting the following afternoon of the entire population of the town. He asked them to bring a cage with several weasels, and a bag with lumps of meat.

When the entire population had gathered in the town square, the sage put the bag of meat on the ground, and opened the cage. Each of the weasels grabbed a piece of meat from the bag, and ran with it to a hiding-place. After a while the weasels came back in search of more meat. The sage put the weasels back in the cage then he went round the square blocking up all the places where the weasels had hidden.

When there was nowhere left for the weasels to hide, the sage opened the cage again. The weasels grabbed more meat from the bag, and ran off. But when they found that all the hiding places were blocked up, they brought the meat back.

The sage concluded: "If none of you ever receives stolen goods, then no one will steal anything." From that day

◆

onward robberies in the town ceased – and the judge and
the constables had nothing to do.

Hasidic

◆

◆

Fish in the river

Two men were strolling along a river. One said to the other: "Look how the fish dart about in the water as they please. You can see that they're enjoying themselves." The other man replied: "You're not a fish. So how do you know what fish enjoy?" The first man retorted: "You're not me. So you don't know whether I know what fish enjoy." The second man said: "Indeed I'm not you, so I certainly don't know what you know. And for the same reason you don't know what fish enjoy."

The sage was also near the river, and overheard the two men's argument. He could also see that their faces were now red with irritation at one another. "May I intervene?" he asked. Both men nodded.

The sage turned to the second man, and said: "Let's go back to your original question. You asked your friend how he knows what fish enjoy. You didn't ask whether he knows what fish enjoy. So you already assumed that a human being has some understanding of other creatures."

The sage then turned to the first man, and said: "You told your friend that he doesn't know what you know. So you already assumed that our understanding of one another is limited."

The sage concluded: "Your two views are quite consistent with one another. So either you are both wrong, or you are both right." The two men smiled at the sage, and then smiled at one another.

Taoist

◆

◆

A scholar in a storm

The sage was on a small ferry crossing an estuary. In addition to the boatman who was rowing, there was also a scholar who was extremely proud of his learning.

"Tell me," the scholar asked the boatman, "have you ever learnt how to read the ancient languages?" "No," the boatman replied. "Then half your life has been lost," the scholar declared.

When they were half way across the estuary, there was a sudden storm that was extremely violent. The water became very rough, and wave after wave broke over of the boat, so that it started to fill with water.

"Tell me," the sage asked the scholar, "have you ever learnt how to swim?" "No," the scholar replied, his face white with fear. "Then the whole of your life may soon be lost," the sage declared.

Just as the boat was about to sink, the storm subsided and the boatman was able to row the boat safely to the shore. The scholar ceased to be proud of his learning, and began to admire the practical skills that other people possessed.

Sufi

◆

A home for the elderly

There was a merchant whose business was quite small compared with many other businesses in his town. But, unlike most other merchants, he found no pleasure in his wealth; he was happy to live in a small house and eat simple food. As a result he accumulated a large amount of money.

There were many elderly people in the town who were very poor. So he decided to build a large house in which they could live. The house was very beautiful and comfortable, and almost every old person in the town came to live there. The construction of the house took all his money; and he set aside the annual profits of his business to provide food. In the morning he gave the old people three ladles of rice, and in the evening he gave them four ladles of rice – with a lentil sauce to go over the rice. This was all he could afford and, besides, his doctor told him that it was the right amount for the old people's health.

At first the old people were very happy and contented and the merchant took great pleasure in visiting them. But after several months they began to complain about the food. "We want four ladles of rice in the morning, not three." The merchant was very annoyed at this. "How ungrateful they are!" he said to himself. And he stopped going to visit the house. With each month that passed, the complaints grew louder and the merchant became angrier. Eventually he found himself hating the old people, and he regretted having built the house.

The sage arrived in the town, and he heard about the unhappiness in the home for the elderly. He went to visit the merchant, and offered to try and make the old people happy again. "You can do what you like," the merchant said, "provided it doesn't cost me any more money."

◆

◆

The sage then asked the old people: "Are you sure you want four ladles of rice in the morning?" "Yes!" they shouted with a single voice. So he instructed the cook to give them four ladles of rice in the morning, and three in the evening. The old people were delighted that their wish had been granted, and thanked the sage profusely. "Don't thank me," the sage said; "thank the merchant – he pays for the rice." So they wrote a letter of thanks to him.

The merchant was very relieved and pleased, and started visiting the old people again. The sage said to him: "When people depend on you, give them what they want – so long as you can afford it. And don't expect gratitude, just accept it when it comes."

Taoist

◆

◆

A stolen ornament

The sage was staying at an inn. Early in the evening the innkeeper's wife noticed that a silver ornament had been stolen from her room. Her grandmother had given the ornament to her on her wedding-day, so it was especially precious. She rushed to her husband in floods of tears, and begged him to find the thief.

The husband assumed that one of the guests was the thief, but had no means of telling which one. Believing the sage to be wise as well as honest, he asked for his help.

The sage watched all the guests with great care. He noticed that one of the guests left a cloak in the washroom. The sage remained in a corner of the washroom – behind a large tub, so he could not be seen. Then he observed people as they came in. One young man washed his hands, and then wiped them on the cloak.

The sage pointed out the young man to the innkeeper. "He is the thief," the sage said. "He has no respect for other people's property." So the innkeeper went into the young man's room, and found the silver beaker in his bag.

Hasidic

◆

◆

The τRiuɑph oϝ Light

Two men, whose farms were next to one another, were constantly arguing. But their wives were close friends; and they longed for the arguments to stop. The sage was passing through the neighborhood; and the two wives asked him if he could turn their husbands from enemies into friends.

The longest running argument between the two men concerned an old barn that stood on the boundary of their two farms; each man claimed that it belonged to him. The sage went to the two men, and said: "Let us have a competition. We shall divide the barn into three equal parts; and in the course of a day, from dawn until dusk, we shall see which one of us can fill his part the fullest. We can use anything we like – vegetables, manure, or whatever. If one of you wins, the winner can take full ownership of the barn; but if I win you must promise never to argue again."

Each man was convinced that he was stronger than the other, and so would win, so they both eagerly agreed. A day was set for the competition and at dawn on that day people from all over the region gathered at the barn to watch. As the sun started to rise, the mayor of the local town beat a drum – and the competition begun. Each man started rushing round his farm collecting everything he could – bales of straw, tools, boxes of fruit, as well as vegetables and manure – and piling it into his part of the barn. The sage did nothing; he just sat and watched them.

Twelve hours later, as the sun started to set, the two men were utterly exhausted, and their parts of the barn were only half full. The sage's part was empty. As darkness fell, the sage walked into his part of the barn, took a candle from his pocket, and placed it on the ground; then he lit it. The flame of the candle filled the barn with light, right up to its

◆

rafters.

"Light has triumphed," the sage declared, with a broad smile on his face, and the crowd applauded and cheered. The sage took each man by the right hand, and put the hands together. The two men, their faces dripping with sweat, stared at one another – and then they embraced.

Celtic

◆

Violent entertainment

A king took great pleasure in watching cockerels fighting. He purchased the finest cockerels in the land, and employed a man to train them in the art of killing other cockerels. At his invitation wealthy merchants and landowners, who also trained cockerels for fighting, came to the king's palace with their cockerels and the king and his guests watched the birds pecking and scratching one another to death. The king also invited the kings of other lands to bring their cockerels and on these occasions the fights were held amid great ceremony in the palace garden, with the entire population of the capital city attending the event.

The sage came to the capital city just as the king of another land was arriving and he attended the fight between the two kings' birds. To the local king's fury, the visiting king's birds were victorious. So the king dismissed his trainer, and issued a message to his people saying that he wanted a replacement.

The sage went to the palace, and said to the king: "I should like to become your trainer of cockerels. If you employ me, I can promise that your cockerels will be supreme." "Very well," the king replied, "I shall give you three months to fulfill your promise. At the end of that time another king is coming with his cockerels – and I do not want to be humiliated again."

After a month the king was anxious to hear how his cockerels were faring, and wanted to see a fight between two of them. So he summoned the sage, and asked whether the cockerels were ready. "No," the sage replied, "at present they just strut around, showing off their size and strength."

After a second month the king again summoned the sage, and asked whether his birds were ready. "No," the sage replied, "at present they just enjoy showing aggression, even

◆

to their own shadows."

Finally after three months the other king arrived. A great stage was erected in the palace garden, and the entire population of the city came to watch. The visiting king's trainer put the first cockerel on the stage. The bird strutted up and down, pecking and scratching the air, and clucking loudly. Then the sage put his first cockerel on the stage; the bird stood still, like a statue carved in wood.

The other cockerel tried to frighten this motionless bird by charging at it but the bird remained absolutely still. The other cockerel clucked at it, and then pecked and scratched but the bird did not move. So the other cockerel marched off the stage in disgust – and so the local king's cockerel was declared victorious. The local people roared with delight.

The visiting king's trainer put cockerel after cockerel on the stage, each more aggressive than the last. The sage's cockerels all remained motionless – and in every case the visiting king's cockerels left the stage.

At first the local king was pleased at his victory. But the following day the sage went to the king, and said: "You have discovered that the path to true victory involves no violence, no glory – and no entertainment at the expense of others." The king abandoned the fighting of cockerels and he also became much gentler and wiser in his rule.

Taoist

◆

A melon in winter

A wealthy landowner, who lived in a large mansion, admired the sage's wisdom and he imagined that, if he could persuade the sage to live with him in his mansion, he might become wise – and perhaps also acquire peace of mind. So he offered the sage the most luxurious room and, as it was winter and the weather was especially cold, the sage was happy to accept.

The landowner was mean and merciless toward the families on his estate. He charged them a high rent, and demanded that they pay it in full even in years when the harvest was poor – and if they failed to pay, he evicted them.

One morning a very old man, who had lived on the estate all his life, trudged through the snow carrying a large yellow melon. He knocked at the door of the mansion and when a servant opened it, the old man asked to see the landowner. The servant went to the landowner, who was sitting with the sage beside a large open fire, and told him of the old man's arrival. The landowner ordered the servant to send the old man away; but the sage insisted that he invite him in.

"Ever since you inherited this estate from your father," the old man said to the landowner, "I have hated you for your meanness and lack of mercy. But soon I shall die, and I want to cleanse my heart of all hatred. So I have brought you this melon that I grew last summer, and that I have stored carefully in straw. I offer it to you as a sign of friendship."

The landowner had not eaten melon since the summer, and his mouth watered at the sight of the large yellow fruit. So he took it, then ordered the old man to leave.

The landowner cut a slice from the melon, and gave it to the sage on a silver plate. The sage ate it with relish,

◆

commenting on its exceptional sweetness. The landowner cut a slice for himself. But as soon as he tasted it, he spat it out in disgust. "It's rotten," he exclaimed. "How can you possibly say it's sweet?" "It was given with love," the sage replied, "and love can make all things sweet."

The next morning the sun was shining and the snow had melted. "It is time for me to leave," the sage said to the landowner. "Remember what the melon taught you, and you will be wise – and your mind will be at peace." The landowner then rode round his entire estate, telling the families that they need only pay as much rent as they could afford.

Sufi

◆

A dispute over meat

A woodcutter went into the forest each day to collect firewood. One day he encountered a deer. The deer was so frightened that it did not move. The woodcutter struck it and killed it. Since he was unable to carry both firewood and the deer, he decided to bury the deer in a ditch, with the intention of returning later to collect it.

The next day the woodcutter went back to the forest, but could not find the ditch where he had buried the deer. Eventually he concluded that he must have dreamed the whole incident. That evening he mentioned this in his village. A few days later a neighbor went to the forest in order to search for the dead deer and, after several hours looking in ditches, he found it. He brought it home, cut it in pieces, and sold the pieces to the people of the village.

When the woodcutter realized that his neighbor had found his deer and sold it, he was furious. He went to the neighbor, and said: "I killed that deer; so I should have the money which you have received for its meat." But the neighbor refused to hand him the money. It so happened that the sage was staying nearby; so they went to him to resolve their dispute.

After he had heard the full story, the sage said to the woodcutter: "If you really caught the deer, you were wrong to think that you dreamed of catching it. If you really dreamed that you caught the deer, you are wrong now to claim the money for it. It seems that you are unable to distinguish between dreaming and waking."

Then he said to the neighbor: "When you heard the woodcutter tell the story of the deer, you realized that he was confused about waking and dreaming; so you took advantage of his confusion by going in search of the deer.

◆

It seems that you distinguish too clearly between waking and dreaming."

The sage then passed judgment: "Since the woodcutter cannot distinguish between waking and dreaming, he would not know whether the money was real or not. Since his neighbor distinguishes too clearly between waking and dreaming, he regards money as more important than it is. Therefore the money must be handed to me, and I shall give it to the poor."

Taoist

◆

◆

Welcome for a singer

A king invited to his kingdom a certain singer, who was reputed to have the most beautiful voice in the world. And he invited all his subjects to the royal palace to hear the singer perform.

The sage was staying in the kingdom, and the king sought the sage's advice on how he should welcome the singer. "Should I meet him at the city gate dressed in my finest robes," the king asked, "and ride with him through the city on a golden carriage?" "No," said the sage, "let you and your son wear the simple clothes of servants, and carry him through the city on a chair."

When the singer arrived at the city, he was cross that he could not see the king in his royal robes. "Perhaps the king will greet me when I reach his palace," he said to himself. And he climbed onto the chair.

When he arrived at the palace, the king and his son put down the chair. The king then bowed low to the singer, and said: "Welcome to my home." "So you are the king!" the singer exclaimed in astonishment. "I look upon myself as your servant," the king replied.

The singer was overwhelmed by the king's humility, and bowed to the ground at his feet. That evening the singer sang more beautifully than he had ever done before.

Sufi

◆

◆

A beautiful scratch

A wealthy merchant owned a large and flawless diamond; it was his most treasured possession, and he showed to everyone that came to visit him. But one day, as he was lifting it up for a visitor to see, he accidentally dropped it, and it fell to the floor. It then rolled out of the front door, bounced down several steps outside, and came to rest on a gravel path. The merchant chased after it and when he picked it up, he saw that it was deeply scratched.

He summoned all the diamond cutters in the city, and asked them to restore it to its former state. But they all said that the scratch was so deep that it could never be removed. The merchant plunged into the deepest misery.

The sage passed through the city, and heard about the merchant's plight. He went to the merchant's house, and said: "If you will lend me your diamond for a day, I shall restore your happiness." The merchant at first feared that the sage intended to steal the diamond; but the sage said that he was willing to allow the merchant's servants to follow him wherever he went. So the merchant lent him the precious gem.

The sage took the diamond to the finest diamond cutter in the city. He instructed the diamond cutter to engrave a rosebud above the scratch, so that the scratch appeared as its stem. The diamond was now more beautiful than ever – and the scratch formed part of its beauty. The sage returned the diamond to the merchant, who was overjoyed.

Hasidic

◆

◆

Honey from the pot

An old woman came to visit the sage. "I am in despair," she exclaimed. "Why?" the sage asked. "My son spends all our money on honey," she replied, "and he eats it straight from the pot. Now he is horribly fat, and we are penniless."

The sage went to see the young man, who told him that he liked honey so much that he could not stop eating it. The sage smiled, and said that he would return in a month. The sage now began to eat the same amount of honey as the young man and after a month he too was horribly fat. Then he returned.

The young man was astonished at the sage's appearance and he was even more astonished when the sage told him the reason. "Do you like honey?" the young man asked. "I like it very much," the sage replied. "In fact, I like it so much that I can now hardly resist it." The young man smiled and the sage said that he would return in another month.

The sage now stopped eating honey; and after a month he was back to his normal size. The young man could hardly believe his eyes. "Now I know that it's possible to stop eating honey," the sage said. The young man never ate honey again.

Celtic

◆

Home town

An old man was constantly moaning to his wife and to his neighbors about the town in which they lived, comparing it unfavorably with the town in which he had grown up. Day after day he moaned: "My home town was much cleaner, its buildings were much finer, and the atmosphere much purer."

The sage passed by, and the old man's wife asked him if he could stop her husband from moaning. "I'm so weary of it," she declared, "that if it continues much longer, I'll have to leave him." "When did your husband last visit his home town?" the sage asked. "He hasn't been there since we married fifty years ago," the woman replied.

The sage went to the old man, and said: "I have heard that your home town is very clean, its buildings are very fine, and its air remarkably pure. Will you come with me to visit it?" "I should happily come," the old man replied, "but I have forgotten the way." "Don't worry about that," the sage said. "I have been told the route."

So the next day the two men set off. The sage took the old man to the finest town that he knew. When they arrived, the old man wept with pleasure. "It is just as I said," he exclaimed; "the streets are clean, the buildings fine, and the air is pure."

At dusk they found an inn in which to stay. Over the evening meal they chatted to other people staying in the inn and in the course of the conversation the town was called by a quite different name from that of the old man's home town. "Have they changed the name of this town in the last fifty years?" the old man asked. "No," the others replied, "it's always been the same."

The old man turned toward the sage, and went red with

◆

anger. "You have deceived me," he cried. "If I still had the strength in my arms, I should beat you until you cried for mercy." "No," replied the sage, "you have deceived yourself. You have allowed yourself to think of your home town as you wanted it to be."

The old man returned to his wife; and he never moaned again.

Taoist

◆

◆

EaRThen pitcheRs

A handsome young king wished to become a wise ruler. Yet it perplexed him that wise people tend to be poor and simple, rather than wealthy and noble like himself. So he invited the sage to his palace, and asked him to explain this.

The sage answered with another question: "Why do you keep wine in earthen pitchers?" "How else should I keep it?" the young king asked. "A person of your wealth and rank," the sage replied, "should keep wine in casks of silver and gold." The sage then left the palace. The king was now doubly perplexed, because he could not understand why the sage had raised the subject of wine. Nonetheless he ordered all his wine to be transferred from earthen pitchers to casks of silver and gold.

Within a few weeks the king's wine had turned sour. So he summoned the sage, and demanded to know why he had given such bad advice. "Your majesty," the sage replied, "I wished to show you that the best and finest things are kept in the poorest and simplest vessels."

The king left his palace and abandoned his fine robes, and went to live in a simple cottage, dressing himself in a rough tunic. And as he acquired wisdom, so his people came to respect his rule.

Hasidic

◆

◆

Thoughts of wrestling

A landowner decided that he wanted to become a scholar, devoting himself to the study of philosophy. But, even though he could run his estate simply by receiving a report each morning from his manager and issuing a few orders, people constantly wanted to speak to him. Salesman called at his house wanting to sell new types of grain or machinery, workers called to complain about how the manager had treated them, and neighbors called to discuss local politics. So he never had any peace in which to read his philosophy books and meditate on their contents.

One day he sent a letter to all salesman, workers, and neighbors asking them no longer to disturb him. But they each said to themselves: "I'm sure it's the other callers that annoy him, not me. After all, he always seems pleased to see me." So the same number of people continued to call at his house.

He decided to visit the sage, who was staying in the district, and ask his advice. The sage said: "There is only one reason why people will stay away from you: fear." "I am such a mild man," the landowner replied, "so how can I frighten people." "Fear is in people's minds," the sage said, "not in the object of their fear."

"So how can I put fear into people's minds?" the landowner asked. "Come to me every evening after dark," the sage said; "and let it be known that I am teaching you the art of wrestling. Don't let anyone ever see you, not even your manager. While you are with me, we shall discuss the philosophy that you have read during the day."

The landowner did as the sage suggested. He required his manager to post a written report each day into his house, and he issued written orders. He left the house each evening

◆

after dark, so his shadowy figure was seen on the road to where the sage was staying. And he spread the idea that the sage was teaching him the art of wrestling.

People imagined that his body was now rippling with muscle, and his manner had turned from mildness to aggression. As a result they were so frightened of annoying him that no one ever called and he was able to study philosophy in peace.

Taoist

◆

◆

A nobleman's gold

The sage was staying with a nobleman. The nobleman possessed a huge quantity of gold and though everyone knew of the gold's existence, no one knew where the nobleman kept it.

A group of robbers from a distant town broke into the nobleman's mansion, and found the sage and the nobleman sitting together. The robbers held their swords at the nobleman's throat, and said: "Unless you tell us where the gold is hidden, we shall kill you."

"But if you kill him," the sage interjected, "he won't be able to tell you where the gold is hidden. Why not kill me first? Then he will be so terrified at the sight of my blood that he will answer your question." The robbers could see the sense of what the sage was saying, and turned their swords on him.

Just as they were about to kill him, the sage said: "Perhaps I am the nobleman, and the other man and I changed clothes when we saw you coming. A nobleman's greatest desire is to leave his wealth to his son. So why else should I have invited you to kill me?"

The robbers now did not know which one of the two men to kill and while they scratched their heads in confusion, the sage and the nobleman escaped. They ran through the numerous corridors of the mansion, with the robbers chasing them, until the robbers were completely lost. Then they jumped out of a window, and fetched the police.

Sufi

◆

Chasing the sun

A young man was especially strong and agile, and he prided himself on being the finest fighter in the world. But far from using his power and skill to protect and defend people, he enjoyed making people frightened of him. He picked quarrels with neighbors and with travelers, in order to provoke a fight and since he defeated all his opponents, often breaking their bones, he was regarded with terror.

The sage was passing through the neighborhood, and sat down outside a tavern. The young man saw him, and swaggered up to him. "Who are you?" the young man asked in an aggressive tone. "I am no one in particular," the sage replied. "I just wander from place to place." "And what do you do?" the young man persisted, his voice becoming even harsher. "Nothing in particular," the sage replied. "I just think." "I despise thought," the young man said, spitting at the sage's feet. "Strength is what matters." And the young man flexed the muscles in his arms.

"Is everyone frightened of you?" the sage asked. "Of course they are," the young man replied, his face glowing with pride. "They run away when they see me." "Are animals frightened of you?" the sage asked. "Of course they are," the young man replied, puffing out his chest. "They too run away when they see me."

"Is the sun frightened of you?" the sage asked. The young man hesitated, not knowing the answer. Then blurted out: "Of course it is." "And does it run away from you?" the sage asked. The young man blushed with confusion. "I've never tried chasing it," he replied. "I shall set you a challenge," the sage said. "This evening when the sun is setting, run after it, and see if it sets more quickly."

The young man could not refuse a challenge. That evening,

◆

as the sun was beginning to set in the west, the young man started running toward it. Night fell, and the sage could just see the young man running over the horizon. The sage settled down to sleep.

The following day the young man returned, utterly exhausted. "What happened?" the sage asked. "As I ran toward the sun," the young man said, struggling to catch his breath, "it refused to set. It remained obstinately in the sky. Only when I collapsed with exhaustion did it finally set."

The sage put his arm over the young man's shoulders, and said: "Use your strength and agility to protect the weak and help the needy. Then other people will happily protect you from your own stupidity."

Taoist

◆

◆

Race for land

A landowner was renowned for his kindness to his workers. His estate was vast and he employed several hundred men and women. But he knew them all by name, he paid them good wages, and he provided them with pleasant cottages in which to live. Everyone was content – except one man, who wanted to have land of his own.

This man went to the landowner's mansion, and begged the landowner to grant him some land. "You would hardly notice the loss of a few fields," the man said, "whereas the possession of a few fields would turn my misery into joy." "But if everyone took a few fields," the landowner replied, "the estate would disappear – and the people would no longer be working together."

The man went away with his head bowed. But as the days passed, his desire for land grew even stronger and a week later he returned to the landowner with the same request. The landowner again refused. But the man's desire continued to grow. In fact, the man came to the landowner's mansion every week for a year, begging for land.The sage passed through the region, and the landowner asked him for advice. The sage said to the landowner: "Give the man as much land as he can walk around in one day, from dawn until dusk. But require him to return by dusk to the place where he started, so the circle is complete."

The landowner told the man what the sage had suggested. The man was delighted. And at dawn on the following day the landowner and the man met at a certain spot, along with many spectators, and the man set out as fast as he could.

By midday, when the sun was at the top of the sky, the man felt very pleased with the great distance he had covered. But as the sun descended, his legs grew heavier and his pace

◆

◆

slackened. And when the sun touched the western horizon, he was still a long way from where he started. He could see the landowner in the far distance waiting for him.

The man tried to go faster; but the harder he tried, the heavier his legs became. And as the sun sank below the horizon, the man collapsed. The landowner ran to him, and wiped his face with a cool, wet cloth. "You have been defeated by your own greed," the landowner said. And from then onward the man was content to remain on the estate, working for the landowner.

Celtic

◆

Catching a Fish

A man owned a large factory in which he employed a thousand workers making all kinds of different goods. Although the factory made a small profit, the owner was unable to make the workers operate efficiently. As a result he was constantly anxious that other factories might be able to undercut his prices, and so drive him out of business.

He decided to become more stern and harsh toward the workers. He employed supervisors, who reported to him any worker who seemed to be slacking and he then dismissed the worker instantly. As a result the workers all worked hard. But they took no pride in their efforts, so many of the products were defective; and the factory was a very unhappy place.

Then he went to the other extreme, allowing workers to function at their own speed, and to take rests when they felt tired. The factory became happy, and the quality of the products improved but the quantity slumped.

Finally the factory owner went to the sage, and asked his advice. The sage took three fishing rods and some bait, and led the factory owner to a river. He gave a rod to the owner, putting some bait on the line, and told him to cast the line into to water. When a fish took the bait, the sage shouted: "Pull with all your strength." The owner pulled on the rod with all his strength – and the rod broke.

The sage gave the owner a second rod. When a fish took the bait, the sage whispered: "Let out the line gently." The owner let out the line until it was fully extended – then the line slipped from the rod, and the fish swam away.

The sage gave him the third rod. When a fish took the bait, the sage said in a normal voice: "Pull the rod upward with exactly the same force as the fish pulls it downward." The

◆

◆

rod remained unbroken, and the fish could not escape. Eventually, when the fish was utterly exhausted, the owner was able to pull it ashore without effort.

The sage asked the owner to take the fish off the line, and throw it back in the river. As the owner did so, the sage said: "When your workers are inclined to act as you don't want them to act, pull in the opposite direction with exactly equal force." Soon the factory was producing goods of the highest possible quality in the largest possible quantity, wages and profits soared, and the owner and the workers alike were happy.

Taoist

◆

◆

Unwelcome visitors

A merchant, who over many years had accumulated a large amount of wealth, grew weary of all the people that visited him. Poor people came begging for money; and rich people came in the hope of doing business with him, and thereby become even richer. The merchant simply wanted to be left alone, so he could conduct his business quietly, and devote his spare time to studying philosophy.

The sage passed through the town where the merchant lived, and the merchant told him of his plight. "I shall tell you the solution to your problem," the sage said, "so long as you agree secretly to give all your profits to the local hospital." The merchant agreed to the condition.

"When a poor person comes to your door," the sage said, "offer him a loan. And when a rich person comes, demand a loan."

The merchant took the sage's advice, and soon no one came to his door apart from those he invited. Not only was he now able to study philosophy, but also during his hours of work he could concentrate his entire mind on his business. As a result his profits soared – so the hospital expanded, and could treat every sick person in the town.

Sufi

◆

Preparations for archery

A young man was eager to learn archery. He wanted to become the champion archer in the district, winning the first prize at every contest. So he purchased the finest bow and arrows that money could buy.

But he proved utterly inept: if he aimed at a tree, his arrow might hit a nearby hedge, if he aimed at a hedge, his arrow might fly past the nose of a nearby cow. Eventually he came to the sage in despair, and asked how he could improve.

The sage said to him: "Whenever you wish to accomplish something, you must consider how best to prepare yourself." "How do I prepare myself for archery?" the young man asked. "Go to a local weaver," the sage replied, "and ask to lie under his loom every day for a month. As the shuttle passes to and fro in front of your eyes, strive not to blink." The young man did as the sage suggested, and learnt to control his blinking.

He returned to the sage, and asked: "Am I now ready to resume archery?" "No," the sage replied. "You must catch a flea each day, and attach it to a hair from a horse's tail. As dusk approaches, hang the flea over a window facing west; and watch the flea with the sun behind it." The young man did this every evening for a month. Gradually the flea seemed to grow larger, until it was as big as a cartwheel. And when he looked at other objects, they too seemed very large.

He returned to the sage, and the sage told him he was now ready to resume archery. The young man took his bow with great excitement; and he found he could hit the target with every arrow. When he looked at the target, he could focus his eyes on it without blinking; and it seemed so large that it filled his vision. As a result he won every contest.

Taoist

◆

◆

Old twins

Two brothers, now advanced in years, were identical twins: they had the same appearance, the same manner of speaking, and the same natural abilities. One of them had enjoyed great success, and was wealthy; he lived in a large mansion, and ate the finest meat. The other had suffered numerous failures, and was poor; he lived in a hovel, and ate millet and vegetables.

The successful twin was proud of his achievements, and treated his brother with contempt, accusing him of being lazy. The unsuccessful twin resented his failures, and was bitter toward his brother, accusing him of gaining wealth by dishonest means. Whenever they met, they argued and quarreled.

One day the successful twin said: "Soon we shall both die; so let us be reconciled before it's too late." "Very well," the unsuccessful twin replied, "let us ask the sage to reconcile us." So they went to visit the sage.

The sage asked the successful twin: "When were you happiest?" The successful twin thought for a moment, and said: "When I was a small boy, playing freely in the meadows and the forests, without a care in the world."

The sage asked the unsuccessful twin: "When were you happiest?" The successful twin thought for a moment, and said: "When I was a small boy, playing freely in the meadows and the forests, without a care in the world."

Then the sage said to them both: "Now that you are old, become like children again." So they obtained a modest house, just like the one in which they had grown up, ate the kind of food their mother had given them, and walked together every day in the meadows and forests. They were as happy as children and they died on the same day in each other's arms.

Taoist

◆

◆

Natural treasure

An elderly man had a small farm that was covered with excellent fruit bushes. For many years he had pruned the bushes with great care, and he had pulled up the weeds around them so each year the bushes had yielded an abundant harvest.

But this man had three sons who were lazy. They spent all their time drinking, gambling, and trying to seduce young women. He was anxious that, when he died, they would allow the farm to become overgrown, and they would starve.

The sage passed through the neighborhood, and the farmer asked his help. "You must retire from your farm immediately," the sage said. "Your sons will take over." The old farmer was perplexed, but he did as the sage instructed – he stopped working.

The sage went to see the three sons, and said: "Long ago I was told that in those fields of fruit bushes there is great treasure – enough to feed and clothe you for the rest of your lives." The young men were excited at the prospect of finding treasure. So they immediately started digging around every fruit bush; and where the branches of the bushes were in their way, they pruned them back.

As a result of their digging and pruning, the bushes yielded the heaviest harvest ever. They picked the fruit, and took it to the nearby market, where they sold it for more than enough money to feed and clothe themselves for the following year.

The sage met them at the market; in fact he had secretly followed them there. As they were putting their money in bags, he said to them: "I see that you have found the treasure." At first they looked baffled – and then they understood.

◆

The three young men continued to work hard and they each had ample funds to marry and have children. And their father died in peace.

Sufi

◆

The death of a son

A husband and wife had a son whom they loved dearly. At the age of twenty this son fell down a well, and died. The husband and wife were overcome with grief.

As the weeks and months passed the wife became calm, and she was able to resume her normal activities. But the husband continued to grieve. During the day he sat in his house and wept, and during the night he walked through the nearby forest, beating his fists against the trees. He failed to sow seeds in the spring, and his fields were overrun with weeds. His wife tried to comfort him, but her words and embraces merely deepened his sadness. So she sent a message to the sage, begging him to come and speak to her husband.

The sage said to the man: "Cast your mind back forty years to your own childhood." The man did so and his mind filled with memories of himself and his friends playing games. Then the sage said: "Cast your mind back twenty-five years, to the time when you and your wife first married." The man did so and his mind filled with memories of new love.

The sage concluded: "In those days you had no son, and now once again you have no son." The man stopped grieving, and went to his fields to pull up weeds.

Taoist

◆

◆

Passage of life

A young woman said to the sage: "I feel sorry for old people." "Why?" asked the sage. "Because most of their life is behind them, and they will soon be dead."

"So do you have any plan to avoid this unhappy state yourself?" asked the sage. "Yes," the young woman replied; "I intend to die while I am still young." "Then," said the sage, "most of your life is already behind you."

Hasidic

◆

Children in a burning house

There was a nobleman who had ten children. His wife had died at the birth of the youngest child. They lived in a large mansion that was very old. It had only one door, and the windows were just narrow slits. The nobleman was a rather mild man with a soft voice, whom his children habitually ignored.

One day a fire broke out in the mansion, and it quickly spread through the rooms of the mansion. The children were all playing in a room at the other end of the mansion from the door. The noble rushed to the room. "The mansion's burning," he exclaimed as loudly as he could, "you must escape before you are burned to death." But the children were so engrossed in their game that they paid no attention. He repeated himself, but still they ignored him.

The nobleman rushed through the flames to the door, and out into the garden. He was tearing his hair in desperation. Meanwhile a crowd had gathered to watch the fire; and the sage was in the midst of the crowd.

When the sage saw the nobleman, he ran over to him in order to comfort him. The nobleman told him that his children were still in the mansion, and had ignored his call. "Not only am I losing my beautiful home," he cried, "but I'm losing my children as well"

The sage asked the nobleman for directions to the room where the children were playing. Then he ran into the mansion. When he reached the room, he said to the children: "Your father has purchased lots of wonderful new toys for you. They're out in the garden, so come and look."

The children immediately left their game and followed the sage. He led them through the flames to the door, and out in the garden. Their clothes were scorched, but otherwise

◆

they were unharmed.

The children hugged their father and then hugged the sage, thanking him for saving their lives. "You believed a lie from me, a stranger," the sage said, "but you ignored the truth from your father."

During the following year the nobleman employed a hundred workmen to rebuild the mansion. And for the rest of their lives his children always listened carefully to what he said – and as a result learnt such wisdom as he possessed.

Taoist

◆

A perfect reflection

There were two artists in a town, and each claimed to be better than the other. Whenever they met in the street or in a tavern, they started to argue about their relative merits.

The sage came to the town, and heard the artists arguing. He went up to them, and said: "I am equal to both of you; and this means that you are both equal to one another." The two artists stared at him in disbelief and with one voice they said: "Prove it!"

The sage persuaded the shopkeepers in the town square to erect two boards facing one another in the middle of the square, and to provide paints of every shade. The sage invited to two artists to come to the square. "Let each of you paint on half of one board," he said, "and I shall paint on the other board. Then let the people judge between us." The two artists accepted the challenge.

The two artists and the sage worked for several days on their boards. One artist painted a picture of a lush valley, while the other artist painted a lofty mountain. The sage, however, put layer after layer of silver paint on his board and when each layer had dried, he polished it thoroughly before adding the next layer.

Finally after a week both the artists and the sage agreed that they had finished; and they invited the people of the town to come and judge their work. The people admired both the picture of the valley and the picture of the mountain. Then they turned to the sage's board – and saw a perfect reflection of them both.

When people had finished looking at the boards, the sage asked them: "Is my work equal to their work?" And they all answered: "Yes." Then he turned to the two artists, and said: "A work of art is a reflection of a person's vision. And one

◆

70

person's vision is as good as another's."

The two artists never quarreled again, and instead they admired one another's paintings. Meanwhile the two boards remained in the town square for everyone to admire.

Sufi

◆

◆

Green salve

The wealthiest family in a certain town made their fortune by bleaching silk. Makers of silk throughout the region brought their unbleached silk to this family, who returned it to them perfectly white. The family employed most of the people in the town, and paid very low wages – so the family's wealth grew even larger.

The sage arrived in the town, and saw the misery of the people. He went to visit the factory, and observed the people working. He noticed that at the end of each day the people covered their hands in a green salve, which prevented the skin on their hands becoming sore from the bleach.

So the sage approached the head of the family, and said: "I should like to have the recipe for your green salve." "The recipe is secret," the head of the family replied; "it was invented by one of our ancestors, and has been passed down from eldest son to eldest son ever since." "If I were to pay you a hundred silver coins," the sage asked, "would you sell me the recipe?" The man's eyes sparkled at the thought of the coins. "I shall consult the other members of my family," he said, "and I shall give you my reply tomorrow morning." The sage knew that the family's greed would compel them to sell him the recipe.

That evening the sage called a secret meeting of the people of the town, and said to them: "If you each give me one silver coin, I shall make you rich, and make the wealthy family poor." Although a single silver coin represented a large portion of each family's savings, they decided to take a risk by trusting the sage. He collected just over a hundred coins.

The next morning the sage went to the head of the family, who said: "I have consulted the other members, and we have

◆

agreed to sell you the recipe for the green salve for a hundred silver coins." The sage handed over the coins, and took the recipe.

The sage then traveled to the capital city of the country, and went to the general in charge of the army. "When you wage war in very cold or very warm places," he said, "the skin on your soldiers' hands becomes so sore that they can barely hold their weapons. I shall march with them, and make a green salve that will prevent this soreness. If it works, I ask you to pay me a hundred silver coins a day." The general agreed – it was a small price for defeating the enemy.

So the sage marched with the soldiers on their next campaign, which lasted a hundred days; and at the end he had ten thousand silver coins. He then gave the recipe to the general for future use, and returned to the town where he had bought it – with the coins stacked in a carriage. He distributed the coins to the people, and also gave them the recipe. With the money they started their own factory for bleaching silk. Thus the people prospered, as the sage had promised, while the wealthy family had no employees, and became destitute.

The sage then gathered the people together, and said: "The wealthy family was made poor by its greed, while you have become rich by your trust."

Taoist

◆

◆

A king's dignity

One winter's day a king and his principal officers decided to go out hunting. It so happened that the sage was staying nearby, and the king invited him to join them.

They spent the entire day riding through forests and up and down hills, chasing deer. To the sage's relief all the deer escaped unharmed and in their frustration the king and his officers ignored the passage of time. When the light began to fade, they realized with horror that they were far away from the palace – much too far to ride before nightfall.

They came to a clearing where a small cottage stood. Smoke was coming from its chimney, and the king, who was now feeling cold, smiled at the prospect of warming himself by an open fire. "We shall spend the night here," the king announced. "Your majesty," the chief officer protested, "it is beneath the dignity of a king to stay with a lowly peasant. We must continue riding through the night."

The sage was also feeling cold. "Your majesty," he said, "the dignity of a king cannot be lowered, but the dignity of a peasant can be raised." The king got down from his horse, and knocked on the door of the cottage – where they all enjoyed a very happy evening and a comfortable night.

Sufi

◆

Adulterated honey

A merchant, who had made a fortune selling honey, came to the sage. Tears were in his eyes, and his hands were trembling. "What is wrong?" the sage asked. "I am wracked by guilt," the merchant replied. "What are you guilty about?" the sage asked.

"Many years ago," the merchant said, "I discovered a method of adulterating honey. So I have been making a profit of five silver coins on every pot of honey that I've sold. But as I grow older, the pleasures of wealth are declining fast, while remorse for my action increases."

"Why don't you confess your guilt to your customers," the sage said, "and give them back your dishonest profit?" "Then I would be hauled before the court, and thrown into prison," the merchant replied. "And besides, my wife would be cast into poverty."

"Very well," the sage said, "I shall suggest an easier solution. But first you must promise to give away to the poor any extra profit that you make." The merchant was puzzled at the idea of making extra profit, nonetheless he willingly made the promise.

"During the next month," the sage said, "reduce the adulteration, so that you make a profit of only four silver coins on every pot of honey. Then come back to me." The merchant reduced the adulteration to the required amount. Customers remarked that the taste of his honey had improved – and his sales increased.

A month later he returned to the sage. "During the next month," the sage said, "reduce the adulteration so that you make a profit of only three silver coins on every pot of honey. Then come back to me." The merchant reduced the adulteration by a further amount. Customers remarked that

◆

the taste of his honey had improved even more – and his sales increased further.

Then at the sage's instruction he reduced the adulteration so his profit was only two coins – and his sales increased even further. Finally he stopped adulterating his honey completely, so the honey was pure, and his profit on each pot was a single coin. The honey now tasted so good that people were coming from far and wide to buy it. His sales were over five times what they had been previously, so his total profit had risen – and every month he gave the extra profit to the poor.

The merchant brought the sage a pot of honey as a token of his gratitude. "Honesty doesn't always bring benefits," remarked the sage with a smile, "but often it does. Besides, if you had always been honest, you wouldn't now be giving money to the poor. So your past dishonesty is now benefiting them."

Hasidic

◆

◆

The GRIEVING WIDOW

An elderly couple lived in a cottage on the edge of a town. Everyone envied them for the harmony of their marriage. They never quarreled, and were always affectionate to one another. But after almost fifty years of such happiness the husband became ill and died.

His widow was overcome with grief. Her children tried to console her, but to no avail. Her neighbors were equally unsuccessful. Even after several months tears continued to roll down her cheeks from morning until night.

The sage passed through the town, and heard about the grieving woman. He went to the town goldsmith, who was a kindly man, and asked to borrow a gold ring. He took the ring to the woman, and said: "I want you to give this to the family that has no sorrows."

The woman set off in search of such a family. She visited every home in the district, and could find no one free of all sorrow. Finally she returned home, and gave the ring back to the sage – who gave it back to the goldsmith. Her grief had gone.

Celtic

◆

◆

A merchant's dilemma

A rich merchant and his wife had a son and a daughter. When they had grown up, the son and daughter both married, and each moved away to another town. Soon afterwards the merchant's wife died and within a year his business failed, so he was destitute. He wrote to his son asking if he could live with him, but received no reply. He then wrote to his daughter, and she wrote back to say that she was too busy to look after him.

The merchant went to the sage, and asked his advice. "Do you wish to start your business again?" the sage asked. "Now that my wife is dead and my children ignore me," the merchant replied, "my zest for business has gone." "Then," said the sage, "you must first concentrate on finding a new wife."

The merchant knew a woman who had recently been widowed, and went to visit her. They developed a warm friendship, which deepened into love. After they had married, the merchant borrowed some money and restarted his business and soon he was prosperous again.

His son and daughter heard about his success, and were anxious that he would bequeath his fortune to his new wife – and she in turn would bequeath it to her own children. So they each wrote to him, expressing their good wishes, and inviting him to stay.

He again went to the sage. "Should I bequeath my fortune to my wife or my children?" the merchant asked. "Go on a journey," the sage replied, "carrying all your wealth – pretend that you intend to invest it in some new venture. Then after a week write to your wife, your son and your daughter, telling each of them that robbers have attacked you, and you have lost everything."

◆

◆

The merchant did as the sage suggested. His son and daughter both replied saying that he should return to his new wife. His wife also urged him to return to her, saying that she would share his poverty, just as she had shared his riches. He not only returned to his wife, but also bequeathed to her all his wealth.

Hasidic

◆

◆

Trees for the Future

An old man came to see the sage, and said: "I have worked hard all my life; and now in my old age I feel useless." "Now you have time to teach the young," the sage replied. "But I am neither wise nor scholarly," the old man said, "so I have nothing to say."

"Do you enjoy walnuts?" the sage asked. The old man was perplexed by this question, but answered: "Yes, I have enjoyed walnuts all my life." "Then you can teach the young by planting walnut trees," the sage said. The old man did not understand the reason for the sage's suggestion, but decided to act on it. He began to plant walnut saplings around fields and since his limbs were stiff and weak, he was very slow.

When he had been doing this for a few days, a young man passed by. "What are you doing?" the young man asked. "Planting walnut trees," the old man replied. "But you will never see the walnuts in your lifetime," the young man said. "The walnuts that I have enjoyed throughout my life," the old man replied, "came from trees that people before me had planted. So am planting trees to give walnuts to those who come after me."

The same conversation was repeated in the following weeks and month with many other young people that passed by. And they each found themselves reflecting deeply on the old man's words.

Celtic

◆

A blow on the cheek

The sage arrived in a region where the harvest had been poor for three seasons in a row. As a result the price of food was so high that only the rich could afford to buy enough to feed themselves, while the poor went hungry.

The sage decided to visit the homes of the rich, and ask them for money to provide food for the poor. Most rich people gave something. But a wealthy merchant, who was reputed to have a huge storeroom filled with gold and silver, slapped the sage on the face and the blow was so hard that the sage's cheek began to bleed.

For a moment the sage was dazed. Then, wiping his cheek with his handkerchief, he said: "That blow was clearly meant for me. Now what will you give to the poor?" The merchant was so astonished that he gave five gold coins.

Hasidic

◆

◆

Powerful words

A woman came to the sage in great distress. "My husband is very ill," she said, "and none of the medicines given by doctors make him better." So the sage went with her to her house.

Her husband was lying on a bed and shaking. His children were gathered round him, quietly weeping; and his brother was seated on a chair nearby. The sage began talking to the man, and soon realized that the illness was in his mind. He had become so anxious about providing enough money for his family, that he had collapsed.

The sage turned to the woman, and said: "Let me come each day for a fortnight, and talk with your husband. Then he may recover." "You fool," the man's brother exclaimed, "words can't make him better." He was flushed with anger, and began to sweat.

"If only a single sentence has the power to make you hot and red," the sage replied, "then many conversations can surely heal your brother."

Sufi

◆

◆

The window and the mirror

A successful merchant, as he grew older, became more and more unhappy. He was perplexed by his own misery, and said to himself: "I have every luxury that money can buy. Yet nothing gives me pleasure any more. How can this be?" It so happened that the sage was staying in the town so he invited him to his house to his mansion to ask his advice.

When the sage arrived, he noticed a large window looking out onto the town square, and also a mirror hanging on the wall. The sage took the merchant by the hand, and led him to the window. "What do you see?" the sage asked. "I see people," the merchant replied. Then the sage led him to a mirror, and again asked: "What do you see?" "I see myself," the merchant replied.

The sage said: "In both the window and the mirror there is glass. But the glass in the mirror is covered with silver and as soon as silver is added, you cease to see others, and just see yourself."

Later that day the merchant wandered through the town. For the first time he forgot about his own needs, and saw the needs of others. He decided to share his wealth with others, and kept only enough to feed and clothe himself. His misery disappeared, and he was happy.

Hasidic

◆

Dreams of change

A landowner with a large estate treated his workers harshly, compelling them to toil from dawn to dusk each day without rest. One of his workers was weak and frail, and the landowner treated him more harshly than the rest. Whenever this worker was unable to perform a particular task, such as lifting a sack or digging a ditch, the landowner accused him of slacking, and beat him with a stick.

The sage passed through the estate. He observed what was happening; and at dusk he went to the weak worker's tiny hovel, asking to stay the night with him. During the evening the weak worker told the sage of his troubles. The sage said: "Just before you fall asleep at night, imagine yourself leading a life of pleasant labor and ample rest, then in your dreams you will experience this life." That night the weak worker did as the sage advised. As a result the night was pleasant and when he awoke he felt better, because he found himself thinking that one day his dream would be realized.

At dusk the following day the sage went to the landowner's mansion, and asked to stay. Late in the evening, just before it was time to go to bed, the sage said to the landowner: "Imagine yourself as one of your workers – such as that weak worker whom you beat with a stick." That night the landowner dreamt of being the weak worker. He awoke in the small hours screaming and sweating. He found himself wondering if some financial disaster might overwhelm him, forcing him to become a worker on someone else's estate and, since he was too weak to lift sacks or dig ditches, he would be constantly beaten for slacking. His body became so tense that sleep was impossible and when dawn broke, he wandered gloomily round his estate, convinced that soon he would lose it.

◆

◆

The sage now left the estate. During the following month the weak worker was happy: his nights were pleasant, and his days full of hope. But the landowner was miserable: his nights were spent tossing and turning, and his days were filled with dread.

Then the sage returned, and invited the two men to sit with him under a tree. He asked them: "Which of you is better off: the worker, with pleasant nights and hopeful days or the landowner, with restless nights and fearful days?" They both knew the answer.

The landowner became kind to his workers, requiring them only to perform tasks they could manage, and giving them ample time for rest. And the weak worker, along with all his comrades, now enjoyed working on the estate.

Taoist

◆

A generous inheritance

A landowner, whose estate included many villages and farms, was dying; and he had no children or other relatives to whom the estate should be bequeathed. The sage was passing through the region and the landowner sent a message to the sage, asking him to pay a visit. "To whom should I leave my estate?" the dying landowner asked. "To someone who is shrewd enough to know that generosity brings its own reward," the sage replied.

"But how can I find such a person?" the landowner asked. "How many horses do you have in your stable?" the sage asked in reply. "Seventeen," the landowner replied. "Very well," the sage said. "Let me compose your will." The sage took a large piece of parchment and a pen, and wrote: "Of my seventeen horses, my chief steward will have a half, my head butler will have a third, and my senior cook will have one ninth. The person able to divide the horses in this way will inherit my entire estate." The landowner signed what the sage had written and the sage gave the will to the local lawyer.

When the landowner died, all the people on the estate gathered, and the lawyer read out the will. Everyone tried to calculate how many horses the steward, the butler and the cook should have but no one succeeded. So the lawyer distributed a poster throughout the region, showing the will, and inviting people to offer the solution – and thus inherit the estate.

After several weeks a young man rode up to the lawyer's office. "I have the solution," the young man said. "Fetch the steward, the butler and the cook, and bring them to the stable." When they had gathered, the young man climbed down from his horse, and put it in the stable. Then he said:

◆

"The steward should have nine horses, which is a half; the butler should have six horses, which is a third; and the cook should have three horses, which is a sixth."

So the young man inherited the estate. He managed it with great shrewdness – and hence with great generosity to his tenants. As a result the tenants worked hard, and the estate prospered.

Celtic

◆

◆

Clever tricks

A young man taught himself to walk on stilts. Then he taught himself to juggle. And finally he taught himself to walk on stilts and juggle at the same time.

He went to the royal palace, and performed in front of the king. He walked forward and backward on stilts, while juggling seven swords. The king was so impressed that he gave the young man a bag of gold coins.

Hearing of this young man's success, another young man taught himself to dance on the back of a horse, while the horse galloped in circles. He too went to the royal palace, and asked to perform in front of the king. But the king ordered him to leave, and never return.

This second young man went to see the sage, and told him what had happened. The sage said: "The first young man had no thought of a reward, so he was rewarded. But you thought only of a reward; so you were not rewarded."

Taoist

◆

◆

A beautiful estate

A nobleman lived in a large mansion, which was situated in a beautiful valley. He admired the sage, and invited him to stay in his mansion. One morning the sage suggested that they climb one of the hills overlooking the valley. So the two men set out, accompanied by several of the nobleman's servants.

The nobleman was old, so they walked slowly. When they finally reached the top of the hill, they sat down, and looked over the valley and the mansion. Tears welled up in the nobleman's eyes. "Why are you weeping?" the sage asked. "Soon I shall die, the nobleman replied, "and I shall depart from this beautiful place. If only I could stay alive for ever!" One of his servants echoed his sentiments: "We too love this place so much that we dread the prospect of death."

The sage smiled, and said: "Let us imagine that your father, grandfather, great-grandfather, and all your ancestors had remained alive. The mansion would now be packed with them, and there would be no space for you. So, far from enjoying its splendor and comfort, you would be working in a rice-field and living in a thatched hut. You must die in order that your descendents can have their turn."

A few years later the nobleman caught a fatal illness. He remembered the sage's words, and was content to die.

Taoist

◆

◆

A carpenter's dreams

A man, who earned his living as a carpenter, spent all his evenings reading books. He was able to absorb and remember the ideas and facts that he read, and hence became proficient in numerous different subjects. Eventually he decided that he would like to share his knowledge with others so he went to nearest large town, and became a lecturer in the university.

Unfortunately he had an extremely harsh and rasping voice. When he spoke softly in normal conversation, it caused little offense. But when he raised his voice to deliver a lecture, the sound was so painful that the students put their hands over their ears.

The sage passed through the town, and the students invited him to hear this lecturer, so that he could understand their predicament. The following day the sage went to visit the lecturer in his home. "Last night I had a wonderful dream," the sage said. The lecturer asked him to relate the dream. "I dreamed," the sage continued, "that your voice was clear and pleasant, and that the students enjoyed listening to your lectures." The man immediately went to the head of the university, and resigned his post.

The following day the sage again visited the former carpenter. "Last night," the sage said, "I had another wonderful dream. I dreamed that you were a brilliant writer, and had written many books filled with original ideas." The man immediately started writing books.

Some years later the sage returned to the town, and found that the former carpenter had become a famous writer, producing books filled with original ideas. The sage went to congratulate him on his success. "I owe my success to you," the man replied "You taught me the value of dreaming as well as knowing."

Sufi

◆

A lazy shadow

A young man was constantly active; from the moment he awoke to the moment he fell asleep he did one useful task after another. As a result his body was constantly tense, his flesh was wasting away, and he was frequently ill. His mother and father were worried that he would soon die so when the sage passed through the neighborhood, they asked him to speak to him.

The sage found the young man engaged in some useful task, and asked him to sit down with him on the ground. The sage said to him: "Look at your shadow." The young man looked at his shadow. "What is your shadow doing?" the sage asked. "It is doing what I am doing," the young man replied, "it's sitting and talking to you."

"Does your shadow follow you in everything you do?" the sage asked. "Yes, of course," the young man answered. "So are you the master and is your shadow the servant?" the sage asked. "Yes," the young man replied

The sage said: "From now onward, from the middle of each day until the evening, you must be the servant and your shadow the master. Follow your shadow in everything it does."

Since his shadow had no power to act on its own, the young man was forced to remain still throughout every afternoon. As a result his body became relaxed, his flesh was restored, and he enjoyed good health.

Taoist

◆

◆

Food for clothes

A certain king held great banquets in his palace every evening. But he invited only noblemen and wealthy merchants, who could afford to dress in the finest clothes. He never invited the ordinary people whose clothes were plain and simple. When the sage passed through the kingdom, the ordinary people complained about this injustice.

That evening the sage went to the palace in his normal clothes but the king's servants turned him away. The following day he visited a merchant who was renowned for his kindness, and borrowed from him a fine suit of clothes. In the evening the sage put on the merchant's clothes and went to the palace, and the king's servants bowed to him, and led him to the hall where the banquets were held.

Since he had never seen the sage before, the king was eager to meet him so he beckoned to his servants to bring the sage to the seat next to him. When the food was served, the sage took the food from his plate, and carefully put it down his sleeve.

"Why are you putting your food down your sleeve?" the king asked in amazement. "Your majesty," the sage replied, "it is my clothes that have been welcomed to this banquet, not me."

From then onward the king invited all his subjects in turn to his banquets, regardless of their wealth or rank.

Sufi

◆

◆

A young man's aims

A young man came to the sage, and said: "My parents are ambitious for me. They want me to pursue success in my life. Should I obey my parents in this?" the sage replied: "Let us assume that you live your full span. You have already spent a quarter of that time in childhood, when you are too young to achieve success, and you will spend almost another quarter too old and weak to achieve success. A third of your time is spent asleep, when you can do nothing; and when you are awake, you must spend some time at rest. Eating and drinking absorbs more time. And you fall sick occasionally. So there is very little time left for success."

The young man said: "Should I pursue pleasure instead? Should my aim be to eat delicious food, wear silks and brocades, listen to sweet music, and surround myself with beautiful women?" the sage replied: "If pleasure is your aim, you will constantly be seeking the means of pleasure – the food, the clothes, the music, and the women. So there will be very little time for enjoyment."

The young man said: "Should a high reputation be my aim?" the sage replied: "If you pursue reputation, you will become the slave of those whose respect you seek. You will constantly try to say what they want you to say, and do what they want you to do."

"So what should my aim be?" the young man asked. The sage replied: "Your aim should be to have no aim."

Taoist

◆

◆

Tranquility amid noise

A man lived in a small house with his wife and seven children. His wife enjoyed inviting friends for cake and a chat and his children, like all children, were boisterous. But he loved tranquility. He was too poor to afford a larger house, where he could have a quiet room to himself, so he was becoming utterly distraught.

The sage passed through the town and the man went to him for advice.

"Do you have a goat in your yard?" the sage asked. "Yes," the man replied. "Then you must bring it into the house," the sage said. He did as the sage instructed. But the goat bleated all day and night, keeping the man awake.

So the man returned to the sage. "The noise in my house is even worse," the man said, his eyes red with fatigue. "Do you have any hens?" the sage asked. "Yes," the man replied. "Then you must bring them into the house," the sage said. The man brought in the hens, and the cockerel followed them. But the hens clucked all day and at dawn, just as the man was finally dropping off to sleep, the cockerel crowed.

A week passed, and the man had no sleep at all. Now, almost mad with exhaustion, he went to the sage for further advice. "Go home," the sage said, "and drive the goat, the hens, and the cockerel back into the yard, where they belong."

The man did as the sage instructed. His relief at no longer hearing their various noises was so great that he hardly noticed the voices of his wife and children. And he could now sleep again. He went back to the sage, and exclaimed: "Thanks to you my house is like a palace!"

Hasidic

◆

◆

Three desires

Three travelers arrived at a village. They sat down in the center of the village and started to discuss what kind of refreshment they wanted. "I want something sweet to eat," the first traveler said. "No," the second traveler said, "I want several sweet things to eat," "No," the third traveler said; "I want something to quench my thirst."

The sage was sitting nearby, overhearing their conversation. One of the travelers said to him: "We only have enough money for one kind of refreshment. Will you choose between us?" "Give me your money," the sage replied, "and I shall satisfy you all." So they handed him their money.

He walked over to the village shop, and purchased a bunch of grapes.

Sufi

◆

◆

Constant vigilance

A mayor of a certain town took great pride in having eradicated all violence. So when the sage passed through the town, he went to the mayor to congratulate him. The mayor puffed out his chest, and beamed. Then he told the sage the story of his success: "When I first took office, there were frequent fights in the streets. So I patrolled the streets every day and whenever I saw the first signs of a quarrel, I intervened, persuading both sides to resolve their differences through discussion."

"Do you continue to patrol the streets?" the sage asked. "Oh no," the mayor replied. "The town is now so peaceful that there is no need. So I can spend most of my time at home." "Keeping peace requires constant vigilance," the sage said. "Nonsense," the mayor replied. "People hold me in such esteem that, so long as I am mayor, this town will remain peaceful."

The sage left the mayor, went into a shop that sold honey, and purchased a jar. Then he smeared a large amount of honey on a nearby wall. Soon great swarms of flies descended on the honey. A little later many larger insects arrived to catch the flies. A cat came, and tried to catch the larger insects. A dog passed by and seeing the cat, the dog attacked it.

A young man saw the dog attack the cat, and hit the dog with a stick. The owner of the dog was furious, and punched the young man. Quickly a crowd gathered to watch the fight, some shouting in support of the youth, and some in support of the owner of the dog.

The following day the mayor resumed his daily patrols.

Sufi

◆

The beggar and the merchant

A certain beggar was the poorest person in a town. He dressed in rags, so in the winter he shivered with cold. He pleaded for scraps of food, so he was constantly hungry. He frequently said to himself: "No one in this town can be more miserable than I am."

A certain merchant was the richest person in the town. His mansion was filled with gold ornaments and precious stones and he was so anxious that thieves might break in, that at night he lay awake. His cooks fed him large amounts of the finest food and as a result he was so fat he could barely walk, and he suffered chronic indigestion. He frequently said to himself: "No one in this town can be more miserable than I am."

The sage traveled through the town, and met the beggar in the street. The beggar told him of his plight. "Who is the richest person in this town?" the sage asked. The beggar told him of the fat merchant, and directed him to the merchant's mansion.

The sage visited the merchant, and the merchant told him of his plight. "I can make you happy and healthy," the sage said to him. "Do whatever is necessary," the merchant replied. The sage fetched the beggar and the other beggars in the town, and he brought them to live in the merchant's house. The beggars took it in turns to guard the mansion at night; and they shared the food that the cooks provided.

The merchant could now sleep at night; and he lost weight, so he could walk at a normal pace and digest food easily. And all the beggars had full bellies and warm bodies.

Taoist

◆

◆

A chest of suspicion

A wealthy merchant and his wife lived happily together for many years. Among their many servants the wife had an elderly maid whom she trusted as if the maid were her own mother; and this maid was the only person that she allowed into her bedroom. But the maid eventually died, and the wife had to promote another maid to take her place.

The new maid had a malicious streak; and she envied the happiness of her mistress's marriage. She noticed that her mistress had a large chest that she always kept locked. She asked her mistress if she could look inside, but her mistress refused.

Then she went to the merchant himself. "Your wife has a chest that she always keeps locked," she said. "She won't even allow me to see inside." The merchant looked puzzled. "I wonder," the maid continued, "if she is keeping something secret – something that she doesn't want you to know about."

At first the merchant dismissed this idea. But as the days passed, he found himself constantly thinking about the locked chest, and wondering what is contained. He did not want to ask his wife, as that would make him appear suspicious of her, yet by keeping silent his suspicions grew. Soon he felt such distrust that he could barely speak to her.

His wife, who had no idea of the reason for her husband's behavior, felt that he no longer loved her; and she assumed he must have fallen in love with someone else. This suspicion grew in her mind, so eventually she could hardly eat.

The sage was passing through the neighborhood, and the merchant asked for his help. When the merchant had told him about his suspicions, the sage said to him: "Foolish suspicions must be buried."

The sage went to see his wife, who told him of her

◆

◆

suspicions. "Foolish suspicions must be buried," the sage said. He then lifted up the chest, carried it outside, and took it to the far end of their garden.

The merchant and his wife followed him, and they watched as he dug a deep hole and buried the chest. As the sage put the last clod of earth over the chest, the merchant his wife turned toward one another – and embraced.

Sufi

◆

◆

Valuable merchandise

The sage was on board a ship crossing a sea. The other passengers were all wealthy merchants, taking valuable merchandise to foreign countries to sell at a profit; and they all assumed that the sage was also a merchant.

One evening, when all the passengers were eating dinner together, one of the merchants asked the sage: "What merchandise have you got?" "The most valuable merchandise in the world," the sage replied. After dinner all the merchants went down to the ship's hold to see the sage's merchandise. But when they found nothing, they laughed, and started treating him as a fool.

A few days later a storm of exceptional violence arose, and the ship was blown onto rocks. The ship and all its cargo were destroyed but the sage and the merchants swam ashore. They were in a country that none of them knew but they asked directions from local fishermen, and found their way to the capital city.

The merchants were forced to beg for food. But the sage simply sat in the main square and soon, sensing his wisdom, people came up to him, and asked his advice. Afterwards most of them offered him money and, aware of the plight of the merchants, he took the money and shared it with them.

The merchants now understood what he had meant – that he possessed the most valuable merchandise in all the world.

Hasidic

◆

A call to war

A messenger from the king arrived at a town, and summoned all the people to the town square. The messenger stood on a platform in the middle of the square, and announced that the king had declared war on a neighboring country – and that he wanted young men to come to the capital city and join his army.

All the strong and able-bodied young men in the town were filled with excitement at the prospect of becoming soldiers and fighting battles. And they mocked the weak and disabled young men who would have to stay at home.

The sage happened to be in the town. He climbed onto the platform, and in a loud voice asked: "Which young men are likely to live until old age, the strong who go to war, or the weak who stay at home?" Everyone fell silent. Then a disabled young man spoke up: "People like me."

The sage asked a second question: "Who will become the fathers of the next generation, the strong who go to war, or the weak who stay at home?" Everyone remained silent. Then another disabled young man spoke up: "People like me."

The strong young men discussed the situation among themselves. Within a few minutes they had decided to remain at home, and let the king fight his own wars.

Taoist

◆

◆

The TRUTH OF IGNORANCE

The sage passed through a certain kingdom where the king was a cruel tyrant, constantly issuing decrees, and punishing severely anyone who disobeyed them. Yet he yearned to be wise. When the king heard that the sage was in his kingdom, he summoned him to his palace.

"I want you to teach me all the truth that you know," the king said. "Truth can only be learnt," the sage replied, "it can never be taught." This answer angered the king. "I shall force you to teach me the truth," the king exclaimed. The sage smiled, which angered the king more.

"I require you to give me three statements of truth," the king declared. "If you refuse, I shall execute you." "If I do what you require, will you release me?" the sage asked. "That is for me to decide," the king said. "Therefore," the sage said, "I hope that you will quickly learn the truth." "Start now," the king demanded.

"The first truth," the sage said, "is that you imagine yourself to be a seeker after truth. The second truth is that you only wish to hear the truth as you currently conceive it. The third truth is that you will only know the truth when you know yourself to be ignorant."

The king released the sage. He also stopped issuing decrees, declaring that he lacked the wisdom to tell his subjects how to behave; and he became gentle and kind toward them.

Sufi

◆

◆

The sweetest sound

The sage was staying at the house of a merchant. The merchant was single and he frequently invited two other bachelors to dine with him.

One evening, after they had finished eating, the merchant said: "In my opinion the sweetest sound in the world is the melody of a flute." "I disagree," one of his friends said. "The melody of a harp is the sweetest sound in the world." "Not at all," the third man said. "The violin has the finest tone you can possibly hear." The three men started to quarrel, each man giving reasons for his belief, and dismissing as nonsense the reasons offered by the others.

Finally the sage interjected: "You are all wrong. If you return tomorrow evening, I shall demonstrate for you the sweetest sound in the world. But my host must allow me to make all the arrangements for the meal." The merchant agreed to let the sage arrange the meal; and the two others agreed to come.

The two men arrived, and sat down at the dining table with the sage and the merchant. The two men and the merchant expected the cook to bring in the food immediately, as she usually did. But minutes passed, and the cook did not come. "I have asked her to prepare a very elaborate dish," the sage said with a smile. The men tried to make conversation, but they were so hungry that they could hardly concentrate on what they were saying.

Half an hour passed, and still there was no food. The conversation became more and more desultory. Finally after an hour the cook appeared with two large dishes, and placed them on the table. Then she lifted off the lids, being careful to clink the lids loudly on the rims.

The merchant and his friends beamed with delight at the

◆

prospect of food. "Now you heard the sweetest sound in the world," the sage declared. "It's the clink of dishes in the ears of hungry people."

The merchant and his friends never quarreled again. And they understood the importance of food, so they were always generous to those in their town who had too little.

Hasidic

A robber as king

There was a young robber who used to attack travelers on a certain road, and steal their belongings. The road went through a kingdom where the king was especially cruel to his subjects, taxing them heavily, and punishing them harshly if they criticized him.

One day this robber attacked the sage as he was walking along this road. The sage's only possessions were the clothes he was wearing. He immediately took them off and gave them to the robber. Then he said to the robber: "May you be happy and successful in your occupation."

The robber was astonished by these words of blessing. "Thank you," he said and he handed the clothes back to the sage.

Some months later the sage was again walking along this road. The robber was about to attack him but then remembered who he was. "Your blessing has helped me hugely," the robber said. "I have stolen more goods in the past few months than ever before."

"I am not satisfied," the sage said. "I want you to find several other young men to join you in your occupation, so you can be even more successful." The robber did as the sage suggested, recruiting several other young men as robbers.

Some months later the sage returned. The robber reported that, with the help of his gang, he had enjoyed even greater success. "I am still not satisfied," the sage said. "You must recruit an entire army of young men, attack the royal palace, and steal the entire kingdom."

The young man was now confident that, if he followed the sage's advice, he would be successful. So he formed an army, and attacked the palace. His young followers fought

◆

so bravely and skillfully that they overthrew the king and the young man became king in his place.

The young man summoned the sage, asked his advice on how to rule. The sage urged him to treat his subjects with kindness, and to allow them to speak freely. Soon the people looked upon the young robber as the finest king that they had ever had.

Sufi

Passing on a secret

A king possessed some secret information of great importance. But he found it impossible to keep the information to himself. So he passed it on to his most trusted servant, making the servant promise that he would not pass on the information to any other human being.

But the servant also found it impossible to keep the information to himself. So he went to the sage, and said: "The king has given me some secret information, but I can't keep it to myself. Let me tell it to you, because I know that you will not pass it on." "But then you would be breaking your promise to the king," the sage replied. "So what can I do?" the man asked in desperation.

"You have only promised not to tell any other human being," the sage said, "so you can still pass on the secret to a cow." The servant went immediately into a nearby field where cattle were grazing. When he had told the secret to a cow, he felt much better; and the cow continued happily to munch the grass.

Sufi

◆

Palmistry and magic

A king had a large gold ring, which had been made for the first king of his land many centuries ago, and handed down from one king to the next. This king regarded it as his most precious possession. During the day he wore it on the forefinger of his right hand and during the night he put it in a silver box beside his bed.

One morning he opened the silver box as usual – and found that the gold ring was missing. He was utterly distraught. There were only twelve servants with access to his room, so he was convinced that one of them had stolen the ring but he had no means of telling which. The sage was passing through the kingdom so the king sent for him, and asked his help.

The sage asked to be given a room in the palace. That evening at dinner, when all twelve servants were waiting at the royal table, the sage mentioned to the king that he could read people's palms – and that a person's palm revealed past actions as well as future prospects. The sage said this in a loud, clear voice, so that all the servants could hear.

During the following morning the sage summoned each of the servants to his room, one by one, and said to each servant: "The king has charged me to find the person who stole his ring. So as part of my investigation I am reading the palms of all his servants." As he read each servant's palm he said nothing. But when he had finished, he gave the servant a piercing stare – then dismissed him.

The dishonest servant was now convinced that the sage was aware of his guilt. So in the afternoon he came to the sage, fell on his knees, and begged for mercy. "I have five children to support," he pleaded with tears in his eyes. "Let me return the ring in secret, just as I stole it. I shall never

◆

◆

do anything wrong again." "Very well," the sage said. "You must return it tonight – otherwise I shall ensure that you are severely punished."

That evening at dinner the sage mentioned to the king that he had a magical ability to retrieve lost objects, and return them to the proper place. So when the next morning the king found the ring in the silver box, he assumed that the sage had used this ability – and he rushed to the sage's room to thank him. But during the night the sage had left the palace, and was now on his way to another land.

Thus the servant was caught because he believed in palmistry and the servant was saved because the king believed in magic.

Sufi

◆

◆

The Rich man and the poor man

Two men, one rich and one poor, happened to arrive at the house where the sage was staying at the same moment; both wanted his advice on some personal matters.

The sage invited the rich man into the house first, and he gave him a full hour of his time. Finally the rich man left, and the sage invited the poor man into the house. He gave him only a few minutes.

"This is unfair," the poor man protested. "When you entered the house," the sage replied, "I could see at a glance that you are poor. But as for that other man – I had to listen to him for a whole hour to realize that in reality he is far poorer than you." The poor man went away happy.

Hasidic

◆

◆

Wisdom from cleaning

A king became weary of ruling, and decided to devote the rest of his life to the pursuit of wisdom. He gave up his throne to his son, and went to visit the sage, who was staying in a nearby village.

"Will you help me to find wisdom?" the ex-king asked. "Yes," replied the sage, "but first you must learn how to clean the village street." The ex-king was perplexed but nonetheless he spent every morning cleaning the village street. He put all the garbage in a basket, and carried it to a pit outside the village. When the people of the village saw their former king in the street, they felt sorry for him. "He is not accustomed to menial work," they said to the sage, "let him do something easier." But the sage was adamant.

One morning a rude young man deliberately tripped up the ex-king, causing him to spill his basket of garbage. "If I were still king," the ex-king blurted out in anger, "I should put you in my darkest dungeon." The ex-king then put the garbage back in the basket. The sage heard about the incident. And that evening he said to the ex-king: "Still you are not ready for wisdom."

About a month later another young man tripped up the ex-king. The ex-king stared at him for a moment, then, saying nothing, put the garbage back in the basket. The sage heard about the incident. And that evening he said to the ex-king: "Still you are not ready for wisdom."

A month later a third young man tripped up the ex-king. On this occasion the ex-king did not even look at the young man, but quietly put the garbage back in the basket. That evening the sage said to the ex-king: "Now you are wise."

Sufi

◆

◆

A Jeweled cap

A nobleman invited a group of friends to his mansion for dinner one evening and since the sage was staying in the neighborhood the nobleman invited him to join them. The nobleman was dressed in fine robes, with a jeweled cap on his head.

The subject of beauty arose, and the nobleman and his friends began to discuss why some people are regarded as beautiful while others are perceived as ugly. Each of them put forward a different view, and soon the debate was quite heated.

Then the sage spoke up. "May I borrow your jeweled cap?" the sage asked the nobleman. The nobleman took the jeweled cap from his head, and handed it to the sage. Then the sage beckoned to a servant. "I want you to take this cap," the sage said to the servant, "and place it on the head of someone who is more beautiful than it is."

The servant took the cap and went round the mansion. He placed it on the head of each of the other servants; but the cap itself was more beautiful than any of their faces. Then he placed it on the head of each of the servants' children but again the cap outshone them. Finally he placed it on the head of his own son. "Ah," the servant said, "you alone are more beautiful than the cap."

The servant went back to where his master and friends were dining, accompanied by his son wearing the cap. "Here is someone more beautiful than the jeweled cap," the servant declared. "And who is this boy?" the king asked, pointing to the boy – who in fact was quite ugly. "He is my son, your majesty," the servant replied.

The sage turned to the king and his friends, and concluded: "Beauty lies in the heart of the one who perceives it."

Sufi

◆

◆

An unhappy town

The sage arrived at a large town, and found the people there very unhappy. He asked the reason for their unhappiness. They told him that an extremely wealthy man owned most of the workshops in the town, farmed most of the nearby land, and thus employed most of the able-bodied men – and that this wealthy man paid low wages and demanded hard work.

So the sage went to see the wealthy man, and said: "You are extremely rich. But what use is wealth?" The man replied: "Wealth enables me to exert power over others." The sage asked: "And what use is power over others?" The man replied: "They fear me." The sage asked: "And what use is being regarded with fear." The man replied: "They obey my orders." The sage asked: "And what use is obedience?" The man replied: "They will work as I want." The sage asked: "And what use is such work?" The man replied: "It makes me rich."

That evening the wealthy man reflected on this conversation, and realized how foolish he was. So from the next day onward he paid high wages, and allowed people to work as their strength and abilities allowed.

Taoist

◆

◆

Cat and mouse

The sage saw a woman sitting outside a cottage, and weeping bitterly. "What"s the matter?" the sage asked. "I have five children to feed and clothe," the woman answered, "but my husband spends all our money in the tavern – and is always drunk."

The sage asked her to take him to the tavern, and point her husband out. The sage then told her to go and borrow a black cat from a neighbor, and lock the cat in her house.

The sage went up to the man, and said: "If you continue drinking, you will turn into a mouse." Then the sage left the tavern. The man, who was only slightly drunk, felt a little frightened by the sage's words and for a few moments he stared into his tankard, wondering whether he should give up drinking.

"What's the matter?" another drinker asked. The man told him what the sage had said. "Don't listen to such nonsense," the other drinker said. "Let's have another round of drinks." And the man continued drinking as usual.

By the time the tavern closed late at night, the man was very drunk. He staggered back to his cottage, fumbled for the key to the front door, and let himself in. In the darkness he could see the eyes of the cat staring at him.

"Don't eat me!" he screamed, and ran away from the house as fast as he could. His terror made him sober, and he continued running until he was too exhausted to move another step. He spent the night under a hedge – and he never went to the tavern again.

Celtic

◆

◆

Blindness to the truth

A rich lawyer had only one offspring, an extremely ugly daughter. Although she was destined to inherit all his wealth, no man showed any interest in marrying her. As a result she became very depressed – and the lawyer himself felt that his own happiness would only be complete if she found a husband.

A doctor came to practice in the town where the lawyer and his daughter lived. He soon gained a reputation for his skill at diagnosing and treating illnesses – despite being blind. The lawyer went to visit the doctor, who was single, and invited him to eat dinner at his house whenever he pleased. The doctor soon acquired the habit of dining two or three times a week at the lawyer's house, and became friendly with his daughter.

One day the lawyer said to the doctor in private: "I should regard it as an honor if you were ever to consider marrying my daughter. And I should be happy to build you a large house, and hand over half my fortune." Soon afterwards the doctor proposed to the lawyer's daughter, and they were married.

The doctor and his ugly wife were very happy together. Then one day the doctor received news of a hospital in a distant city that had developed a cure for his form of blindness. He decided to make the journey there.

As he was preparing to depart, the sage came to the town, and heard about the blind doctor and his ugly wife, and about the cure that the doctor was about to seek. The sage went to see the doctor, ostensibly to receive treatment for some minor ailment.

After the doctor had prescribed a suitable medicine, the sage engaged him in conversation about philosophy. In the

◆

course of the conversation the sage remarked: "There are some instances where the inability to see the truth is a blessing." And near the end of the conversation the sage found occasion to repeat the remark.

After the sage had left, the doctor reflected on what the sage had said. Then he cancelled his trip.

Sufi

◆

Two chief ministers

A king appointed a certain man as chief minister. After a few months as chief minister, the man came to the sage, and said: "The king is sometimes cautious and sometimes brave, sometimes calm and sometimes anxious, sometimes gentle and sometimes firm. How should I respond to his changing moods?" "You have a choice, the sage replied. "Either you can adapt your mood to his, or you can make your mood the opposite to his. If you take the former choice, you will benefit; if you take the latter choice, your family will benefit."

The man loved his family dearly, so he decided to make his mood the opposite of the king's. When the king was brave he was cautious, and when the king was cautious he was brave. When the king was anxious he was calm, and when the king was calm he was anxious. When the king was firm he was gentle, and when the king was gentle he was firm. As a result they acted together with moderation, and so ruled with great wisdom.

The king, however, grew weary of his chief minister having the opposite mood to his and he accused him of being perverse. The chief minister admitted that he altered his moods deliberately so the king beheaded him. But the people remembered this chief minister with gratitude and as a result they treated his family with great respect and generosity.

The king appointed another man as his chief minister. After a few months as chief minister, the man came to the sage, and said: "The king is sometimes cautious and sometimes brave, sometimes calm and sometimes anxious, sometimes gentle and sometimes firm. How should I respond to his changing moods?" "You have a choice, the sage replied. "Either you can adapt your mood to his, or you can make your mood the opposite to his. If you take the former

◆

choice, you will benefit; if you take the latter choice, your family will benefit."

The man was ambitious, so he decided to adapt his moods to the king's. When the king was brave he was brave, and when the king was cautious he was cautious. When the king was anxious he was anxious, and when the king was calm he was calm. When the king was firm he was firm, and when the king was gentle he was gentle. As a result their actions were extreme, and they ruled with great folly.

The king, however, was delighted that his chief minister was in such close sympathy with him, and gave him a grand mansion in which to live. The man eventually died and the people were delighted. The king took back the mansion, and the man's family was forced to live in poverty.

Taoist

◆

True ownership

An elderly merchant had accumulated through the course of his life a huge collection of gems – rubies, sapphires, and emeralds. He kept them in a golden cask, which he locked in a safe.

One year there was a terrible famine in the region. People knew about the merchant's collection of gems – and they knew that, if the gems were sold, there would be ample money to buy food from neighboring regions. Several people brought their starving children to the merchant's house, and begged him for a gem in order to save the children's lives but he adamantly refused.

The sage passed through the region and people told him about the miserly merchant. So the sage went to the merchant's house, and said: "I hear that you have a beautiful collection of gems. Would you allow me to see them?" The merchant was a little suspicious. But he had several hefty servants who could seize the sage if he tried to steal the gems. And besides, he had not looked at the gems himself for several years, and thought that he too would enjoy inspecting them. So he welcomed the sage.

Carefully he took the gold casket out of the safe, placed it on a table, and opened the lid. He then spread the gems across the table. They sparkled so brightly that they seemed to fill the room with light. The sage and the merchant stared at them for several minutes. Then the merchant put them back in the casket, and placed the casket back in the safe.

"Thank you for giving me those gems," the sage said. "But I haven't given them to you," the merchant replied indignantly. "They belong to me." "I have had as much pleasure as you from looking at them," the sage replied.

◆

"So there is no difference between us – except that you have had the expense of buying them, and you have the anxiety of protecting them from theft."

Later that day the merchant took out the casket and went round the region on his horse, giving a gem to every household.

Celtic

◆

◆

The mountain path

A certain scholar took great pride in the sharpness of his mind, and he believed that he could solve any problem by means of logic. On one occasion he had to take a long journey. He only knew the first half of the route, but he was certain that he could deduce the second half, and hence reach his destination safely. So he climbed on his donkey and set out.

The first half ended at a small town. He went to the town square, and asked for the most truthful inhabitant and the greatest liar. He thought that, if he asked them both directions to his destination, he would hear from the truthful person the shortest and safest route, and from the liar he would hear the longest and most dangerous route.

The people in the square introduced him to the most truthful inhabitant, and the scholar asked him the best way to his destination. "Take the mountain path," the truthful man said. The people then introduced him to the greatest liar, and he asked the same question. "Take the mountain path," the liar said.

The scholar was perplexed. So he asked several others in the town the best way to his destination. Some said: "By the river." Some said: "Across the fields." And some said: "By the mountain path." So he remained perplexed.

Eventually he decided to take the mountain path; and he safely reached his destination, which was a large town. He went to an inn for food and shelter; and while he was eating, he related what had happened in the small town. The sage was at the inn, and listened to the scholar's story.

When the scholar had finished, the sage said: "Your problem was that you relied only on your own logic. Instead you should have tried to understand the logic of others."

◆

THE WANDERING SAGE

◆

The scholar looked perplexed. The sage continued: "The river is the easiest route, and you could easily have hired a boat; so the liar suggested the mountain path. The truthful man noticed that you had a donkey, making the mountain path easy, and the river impossible."

Sufi

◆

◆

Money for flattery

The sage arrived in a town where there were a substantial number of rich people, a much larger number of poor people, and very few in between. So he decided to devote his time to collecting money from the rich, in order to provide food, clothing, and shelter for the poor. His method was to flatter the rich and he was quite willing to stoop and bow before them.

The poor were grateful for the help that they received from the sage but they were affronted by the sage's method. One day one of them said to him: "These rich people are far inferior to you in wisdom, scholarship, and morality. Surely it is beneath your dignity to stoop and bow before them." The sage smiled, and replied: "I simply follow the order of nature. Cows are inferior to human beings in wisdom, scholarship, and morality. Yet human beings have to stoop and bow before cows in order to milk them."

Hasidic

◆

◆

Medical advice

A wealthy merchant fell ill. He was skeptical about physicians, and at first refused to call one. But after seven days his illness reached a crisis and his family insisted on calling a physician.

The physician examined the merchant and then declared: "Your illness is caused by irregular meals, excessive sexual activity, and anxiety about your business. Therefore if you eat regularly, abstain from sex, and give up your business, you will be cured." Despite his weakness the merchant shouted: "You're a fool! Get out of my house!"

The merchant's family called a second physician, who examined him, and declared: "Your illness was caused by receiving too little vital fluid in your mother's womb, and too much milk at your mother's breast. So it cannot be cured." The merchant exclaimed: "You're intelligent. Stay for dinner."

The merchant's family was now in despair. So they sent a message to the sage, explaining what had happened, and asking him to visit the merchant. The sage said to the merchant: "In rejecting treatment you increase the likelihood of dying from this illness but you also demonstrate your indifference to whether you live or die. Therefore folly and wisdom are equally balanced in you."

The merchant was astonished at the sage's words. He began following the first physician's advice, and within a few days he was cured.

Taoist

◆

◆

Wisdom for a fool

During his reign a certain king had won many battles over his neighbors and as a result his kingdom had expanded hugely, and he had amassed great wealth. He regarded himself as the greatest king on earth. Now he wished to acquire wisdom as well. So he invited the sage to his palace to teach him.

"Your majesty," the sage said, "wisdom is extremely hard to acquire, and involves much pain." "Nonsense," the king replied. "Since I have conquered almost an entire continent, I can easily conquer wisdom. I order you to teach me, or else I shall order you to be executed." "Very well," the sage replied, "but I insist that our class should be held in the main square of your city – then you might succeed." The king readily agreed to this condition, anticipating that his subjects would be astonished at his ease in acquiring wisdom, and hence would respect him even more.

The next day the king rode out of his palace to the main square, where the sage was waiting for him. A huge crowd was waiting. "I shall make a series of statements," the sage said, "and after each statement you must answer, 'I believe you.'" "That sounds easy," the king replied, with a self-confident smirk on his face.

"This kingdom is very large," the sage said. "I believe you," the king replied. "Many people live in this kingdom," the sage said. "I believe you," the king replied. "Its army is very powerful," the sage said. "I believe you," the king replied. "It is ruled by a fool," the sage said. "That is a lie!" the king shouted.

"I told you that wisdom is hard to acquire," the sage said and then he disappeared into the crowd. The king felt so humiliated that he began to become wise.

Celtic

◆

◆

SOURCES

Taoist

Chuang Tzu, Basic Writings, tr. Burton Watson (New York, Columbia University Press, 1964).

Chuang Tzu, The Inner Chapters, tr. A. C. Graham (London, George Allen & Unwin, 1981).

Chuang Tzu, The Book of Chuang Tzu, tr. Martin Palmer and Elizabeth Breuilly (London and New York, Viking Penguin, 1996).

Lieh Tzu, The Book of Lieh Tzu, tr. A. C. Graham (New York, Columbia University Press, 1990)

Yang Chu, The Garden of Pleasure, tr. Anton Forke (London, John Murray, 1912).

Sufi

Nizam al-Din, Morals for the Heart, tr. Bruce B. Lawrence (New York, Paulist Press, 1992).

Rumi, Tales of Mystic Meaning, tr. R. A. Nicholson (London, Chapman and Hall Ltd, 1931).

Sadi, The Rose Garden, tr. Edward B. Eastwick (London, The Octagon Press, 1979).

Hasidic

Montefiore, C. G. and Loewe, H. eds, A Rabbinic Anthology (London, Macmillan and Co., 1941).

Newman, Louis J. and Spitz, Samuel, eds, The Hasidic Anthology (New York, Scribner, 1934).

Ausubel, Nathan, A Treasury of Jewish Folklore (New York, Crown Publishers, 1948).

◆

Celtic

Hyde, D., The Religious Songs of Connacht (London, M. H. Gill & Son Ltd, 1906).

Van de Weyer, Robert, Celtic Parables (London, SPCK, 1997).

Wilde, Lady, Ancient Legends, Mystic Charms and Superstitions of Ireland (Ward and Downey, 1887).

◆